EQUIPPED TO
EVANGELIZE

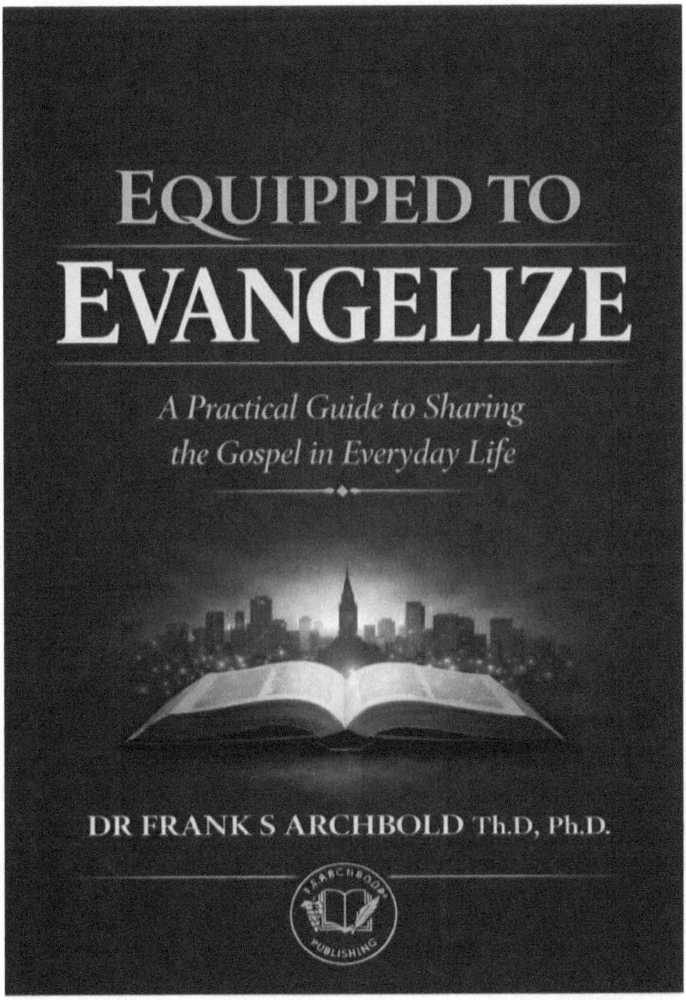

*A Practical Guide to Sharing
the Gospel in Everyday Life*

DR FRANK S ARCHBOLD Th.D, Ph.D.

MINISTRY AND EDUCATIONAL USE

This publication may be used by churches, ministries, Christian schools, discipleship programs, and non-profit religious organizations for **educational and non-commercial purposes**, provided the content is not altered and all copyright notices are preserved. For bulk reproduction, curriculum use, or translations, written permission is required.

DOCTRINAL STATEMENT

The teachings contained in this book are grounded in the Holy Scriptures and reflect the author's theological, pastoral, and evangelistic convictions. They are presented for the purpose of equipping believers, edifying the Church, and advancing the Great Commission of Jesus Christ.

DEPENDENCE ON THE HOLY SPIRIT

This work affirms that effective evangelism is ultimately the work of the Holy Spirit, who guides the witness and convicts the heart. Methods and tools presented herein are intended to serve as instruments under the direction and power of the Spirit of God.

SCRIPTURE REFERENCES

Unless otherwise indicated, Scripture quotations are taken from the **Holy Bible, King James Version (KJV)**. Public domain.

DISCLAIMER

This book is intended for spiritual instruction and discipleship. It does not replace pastoral counseling, professional guidance, or the authority of the local church. Readers are encouraged to seek wisdom, prayer, and accountability as they apply these principles.

PUBLISHING INFORMATION
Published by: **F. S. Archbold Publishing LLC**
First Edition: 2026
Printed in the United States of America

ISBN: 978-1-971265-07-0

TABLE OF CONTENTS

CONCLUSION
Faithful Witness Until He Comes

APPENDICES

- Appendix A — A Simple Gospel Outline
A Ready-to-Use Presentation

- Appendix B — Key Scriptures on Evangelism and the Holy Spirit

- Appendix C — Sample Evangelism Prayers
Depending on the Spirit in Witness

- Appendix D — Small Group & Training Guide
Church and Classroom Use

GLOSSARY
Essential Evangelism Terms Explained

BIBLIOGRAPHY
Recommended Resources for Further Study

ABOUT THE AUTHOR

CERTIFICATE OF COMPLETION

DEDICATION

This work is reverently dedicated first and above all to **Jesus Christ**, the crucified and risen Lord, the Savior of sinners, the faithful Witness, and the eternal Son of God. To Him who left heaven's glory, entered a broken world, bore our sin upon the cross, and rose victorious from the grave— this book belongs. For without Him there is no gospel, no salvation, and no mission. It is also dedicated to the **Church of the Living God**— to pastors, teachers, evangelists, missionaries, and faithful believers across generations who have labored, often unseen, to proclaim the unchanging gospel in changing times.

To those who preach from pulpits and to those who witness quietly in homes, workplaces, schools, streets, and nations— may this work strengthen your faith, clarify your calling, and renew your confidence in the power of the gospel of Jesus Christ. This book is further dedicated to **every believer who senses the call to share Christ yet feels inadequate, hesitant, or afraid**. May these pages remind you that God does not call the equipped— He equips the called. May you learn to depend not on your strength, but on the Holy Spirit, who convicts hearts, opens doors, and brings life where there was death.

Finally, this work is dedicated to **the lost**, known and unknown, near and far— men and women, young and old, who are searching for truth, meaning, and hope. May the gospel reach them clearly, lovingly, and faithfully through the lives of those who are willing to be sent.

"And he said unto them, Go ye into all the world, and preach the gospel to every creature." — Mark 16:15

May this book serve the glory of God, the mission of the Church, and the salvation of souls until the day Christ returns.

FOREWORD
A Call to Faithful Witness in Our Time

The call to evangelize has never changed, but the context in which we proclaim the gospel has. We live in a time of great confusion, spiritual hunger, and moral uncertainty. Many hearts are searching for truth, yet many believers feel uncertain about how—or whether—to share their faith. Fear, distraction, cultural resistance, and a misunderstanding of evangelism itself have caused many within the Church to grow silent.
Yet the command of Christ remains clear.

Jesus did not commission only pastors, missionaries, or evangelists by title. He commissioned **every believer** to be His witness. Evangelism is not a task reserved for the gifted few; it is the joyful responsibility of the redeemed. The gospel was never meant to be hidden within church walls but carried into everyday life—into homes, workplaces, schools, neighborhoods, and nations.

Faithful witness does not require perfection, eloquence, or special training. It requires obedience, love for the lost, and dependence on the Holy Spirit. From the earliest days of the Church, God has used ordinary men and women—filled with His Spirit and grounded in His Word—to transform lives and communities through the power of the gospel.

This book was written to answer a vital need in our time: to restore confidence, clarity, and biblical balance to evangelism. It is not designed to replace prayer, the work of the Holy Spirit, or the life of the local church. Rather, it serves as a practical tool to help believers understand the message they carry, the role they play, and the divine power that accompanies faithful witness.
The urgency of evangelism has never been greater. Souls are eternal. Opportunities are often fleeting. The Church must once again embrace its calling—not with pressure or performance, but with compassion, conviction, and courage.

May this book encourage you to trust God more deeply, to depend fully on the Holy Spirit, and to step forward in obedience. As you do, may you discover that evangelism is not a burden to fear, but a privilege to embrace.

May the Lord use this work to strengthen His Church and to draw many to saving faith in Jesus Christ.

INTRODUCTION
Why Evangelism Matters More Than Ever

We live in a world filled with voices, information, and opinions, yet many hearts remain empty and searching. Technology has advanced, communication has multiplied, and knowledge has increased—but true hope, lasting peace, and spiritual clarity remain elusive for countless people. In the midst of this reality, the message of the gospel has not lost its power, relevance, or urgency.

Evangelism matters because souls are eternal. The gospel of Jesus Christ is not one message among many; it is the power of God unto salvation. It addresses humanity's deepest need—the reconciliation of sinners to a holy God. While cultures shift and methods change, the core mission of the Church remains unchanged: to proclaim Christ, call people to repentance and faith, and invite them into new life through Him.

Yet many believers today feel unprepared or hesitant when it comes to sharing their faith. Some fear rejection. Others feel they lack the right words, sufficient knowledge, or spiritual boldness. Still others assume evangelism is reserved for pastors, missionaries, or those with a special calling. These misconceptions have silenced many willing hearts and left the work of evangelism to a few.

Scripture teaches otherwise. Every believer is called to be a witness. Evangelism is not a program, an event, or a personality type— it is a lifestyle rooted in obedience and love. It flows naturally from a life transformed by Christ and empowered by the Holy Spirit. When believers understand the gospel clearly, walk closely with God, and depend on the Spirit's guidance, evangelism becomes less intimidating and more faithful.

This book was written to address both the **urgency** and the **practical need** of evangelism in our time. It is designed to provide a solid biblical foundation, a clear understanding of the gospel message, and practical guidance for sharing Christ in everyday life. It emphasizes dependence on the Holy Spirit, integrity of character, and compassion for those who are lost.

Evangelism today does not require louder voices or clever strategies—it requires faithful witnesses. God continues to work through ordinary believers who are willing to be used. When the Church embraces its mission with humility and obedience, God brings fruit in ways only He can.

As you read this book, may you be encouraged to see evangelism not as a burden, but as a privilege. May fear be replaced with faith, confusion with clarity, and hesitation with obedience. And may you discover that God delights in using willing hearts to proclaim His saving grace.

Now more than ever, the world needs the gospel. Now more than ever, the Church must be equipped to evangelize.

CHAPTER 1
The Heart of God for the Lost
Understanding God's Redemptive Mission

Evangelism Begins with God

Evangelism does not begin with a command, a method, or a strategy. It begins with **God Himself**. Before believers are called to go, speak, or witness, Scripture reveals a God who seeks, loves, and redeems. Evangelism is not humanity reaching upward toward God; it is **God reaching outward toward humanity**, inviting participation in His redemptive work.

To understand evangelism rightly, one must first understand the heart of God. Without this foundation, evangelism becomes mechanical, guilt-driven, or reduced to religious obligation. When the heart of God is understood, evangelism becomes a joyful response to divine love.

God Is a Seeking God

From the earliest pages of Scripture, God is revealed as One who pursues the lost. After humanity's fall into sin, God's first recorded words were not words of judgment, but of pursuit: *"Where art thou?"* — Genesis 3:9

This question reveals the nature of God's response to sin—not abandonment, but invitation. God moved toward fallen humanity, initiating restoration.

Throughout biblical history, God repeatedly sought those who were far from Him:
- He called Abraham to bless the nations.
- He sent prophets to call Israel back to covenant faithfulness.
- He patiently pursued rebellious people with mercy and truth. Evangelism flows from this same divine initiative.

God's Compassion for the Lost

The ministry of Jesus reveals the depth of God's compassion. Scripture repeatedly describes Jesus as being *moved with compassion* when He encountered people who were spiritually lost, confused, or burdened.

"But when he saw the multitudes, he was moved with compassion on them, because they fainted, and were scattered abroad, as sheep having no shepherd." — Matthew 9:36

Compassion is not passive sentiment; it is love that acts. It sent Jesus into the world. It carried Him to the cross. It continues today through the witness of His people. Evangelism without compassion becomes harsh and ineffective. Compassion without truth becomes incomplete. God's heart holds both love and truth together.

God Desires That None Be Lost

Scripture leaves no ambiguity about God's desire for humanity:
"The Lord is not willing that any should perish, but that all should come to repentance." — 2 Peter 3:9

This does not deny human responsibility or the reality of judgment. Rather, it reveals God's patience and mercy.

Evangelism is fueled not by fear alone, but by love, urgency, and eternal concern. God's desire for salvation explains the urgency of the gospel and the calling of the Church. Time matters. Eternity matters. Souls matter.

Lostness Is a Spiritual Reality

To understand evangelism, one must understand what it means to be lost. Scripture describes lostness not merely as ignorance or moral weakness, but as **spiritual separation from God**.

"For all have sinned, and come short of the glory of God." — Romans 3:23

Lostness is universal. Salvation is not a reward for moral effort; it is a gift of grace. Recognizing this reality humbles the believer and deepens compassion for others.

Jesus illustrated lostness through parables of a lost sheep, a lost coin, and a lost son. In each story, the emphasis is not merely on what was lost, but on the **joy of restoration**.

"Likewise joy shall be in heaven over one sinner that repenteth." — Luke 15:7

Evangelism Reflects God's Nature

When the Church evangelizes, it reflects God's heart. When it neglects evangelism, it misrepresents Him. The Church was never intended to be a refuge that hoards grace, but a mission people who extend it.

Evangelism is not about pressure or performance. It is about **participation**—joining God in what He is already doing. God draws hearts. God convicts. God saves. Believers obey and witness.

Understanding this truth removes fear and restores confidence.

A Call to Align Our Hearts with God's

Before believers learn *how* to evangelize, they must learn *why* they evangelize. Techniques may help, but only love sustains. When the heart of the evangelist is aligned with the heart of God, witness becomes natural and faithful.

Evangelism becomes:
- obedience rather than obligation
- compassion rather than coercion
- faithfulness rather than performance

This alignment prepares the believer for everything that follows in this book.

Reflection Questions
1. How does understanding God's heart for the lost reshape your view of evangelism?
2. In what ways has God demonstrated His pursuing love in your own life?
3. How can compassion deepen both the courage and credibility of your witness?

Personal Assignments

- **Assignment 1 — Scripture Meditation:** Read Luke 15 and reflect on how each parable reveals God's heart for the lost.
- **Assignment 2 — Heart Examination:** Ask God to reveal any attitudes that hinder compassion for the lost and pray for alignment with His heart.
- **Assignment 3 — Prayer Commitment:** Commit to praying daily for at least one person who does not yet know Christ.

Ministry / Small-Group Assignments

Group Discussion
Discuss how churches can reflect God's heart for the lost without compromising biblical truth.

Teaching Activity
Identify biblical examples of God pursuing individuals or nations and discuss their relevance today.

Group Prayer
Pray for renewed compassion, spiritual sensitivity, and obedience in evangelism.

Prayer

Heavenly Father, Thank You for loving us when we were lost and far from You. Thank You for seeking, pursuing, and redeeming us through Jesus Christ. Align our hearts with Yours. Remove indifference, fear, and self-centeredness, and replace them with compassion, obedience, and love. Teach us to see people as You see them and to participate faithfully in Your redemptive mission. May our lives reflect Your heart for the lost, for Your glory alone. In Jesus' name, Amen.

Chapter 1
Reflection & Notes Worksheet
Equipped to Evangelize

Chapter Title: The Heart of God for the Lost
Date: _____

Key Scriptures from This Chapter (Write the Bible verses that stood out most to you.)

_____

_____

_____

_____

_____

_____

_____

Main Truths & Key Insights (What were the most important teachings or ideas in this chapter?)

_____

_____

_____

_____

_____

_____

_____

Personal Reflection (How did this chapter challenge, encourage, or correct your thinking?)

_____

_____

_____

_____

_____

_____

_____

Application to My Life (What changes, actions, or attitudes does God want you to apply?)

_____

_____

_____

_____

_____

_____

Evangelism Focus (How does this chapter help you grow as a witness for Christ?)

_____

_____

_____

_____

_____

Prayer Response (Write a prayer in response to what you learned.

_____

_____

_____

_____

_____

_____

Questions I Still Have (Write any questions you want to study further or discuss.)

_____

_____

_____

_____

_____

_____

Action Step for This Week (One practical step you will take based on this chapter.)

_____
_____
_____
_____
_____
_____
_____

Additional Notes

_____
_____
_____
_____
_____
_____

Discussion Notes / Group Insights:

_____
_____
_____
_____
_____
_____
_____

CHAPTER 2
The Great Commission and the Early Church
Jesus' Mandate and the Book of Acts Model

The Mission Given by Christ

Evangelism is not a human invention or a church growth strategy. It is a **direct mandate from Jesus Christ**. Before His ascension, Jesus entrusted His followers with a mission that would define the Church's purpose until the end of the age.

"Go ye therefore, and teach all nations... teaching them to observe all things whatsoever I have commanded you." — Matthew 28:19–20

The Great Commission is not optional, selective, or reserved for a few. It is the calling of **every believer**. To follow Christ is to be sent by Christ.

Understanding the Great Commission Clearly

The Great Commission contains four inseparable elements:
1. **Go** — a movement outward, not inward
2. **Make disciples** — not merely converts
3. **Baptize** — identifying believers with Christ
4. **Teach** — grounding believers in obedience

Evangelism is therefore not complete at proclamation alone. It begins with proclamation and continues through discipleship.
The authority behind this command is unmistakable:

"All power is given unto me in heaven and in earth." — Matthew 28:18

Evangelism flows from Christ's authority, not human confidence.

The Scope of the Mission

Jesus' command extends to **all nations**, cultures, and peoples. The gospel was never meant to remain confined to one group or region.

"And ye shall be witnesses unto me... unto the uttermost part of the earth." — Acts 1:8

This global vision prevents evangelism from becoming inward-focused or culturally exclusive. Every believer participates—locally, relationally, and globally.

The Book of Acts: Evangelism in Action

The Book of Acts demonstrates how the early Church understood and lived out the Great Commission. Acts is not merely history; it is a **Spirit-inspired model** of faithful witness.

From the beginning:
- the gospel was proclaimed publicly and personally
- believers depended on the Holy Spirit
- persecution did not stop the mission
- ordinary people became powerful witnesses

The Church did not wait for perfect conditions—it obeyed.

Spirit-Empowered Witness

Acts reveal that evangelism advanced not through political influence or human persuasion, but through **Spirit-empowered obedience**.

"And they were all filled with the Holy Ghost, and they spake the word of God with boldness." — Acts 4:31

Boldness was not personality-driven; it was Spirit-produced. The early believers trusted God to open doors, convict hearts, and confirm the message.

Evangelism in Word and Deed

The early Church proclaimed Christ verbally and demonstrated His power through love, unity, and service. Evangelism was holistic— truth spoken clearly, and lives lived consistently.

Acts records:
- preaching in synagogues and homes
- conversations in marketplaces
- testimonies before rulers
- faith lived under persecution

The gospel moved wherever believers went.

Persecution Did Not Silence the Mission

Opposition did not weaken the early Church—it purified and expanded it.

"Therefore they that were scattered abroad went everywhere preaching the word." — Acts 8:4

Evangelism was not confined to apostles. Every believer became a witness. The mission advanced because the Church understood evangelism as identity, not activity.

The Pattern That Still Applies Today
The Book of Acts establishes a timeless pattern:
- Christ gives the mission
- The Spirit empowers the Church
- believers obey faithfully
- God produces the growth

This pattern remains unchanged. Methods may adapt, but the mission does not.

A Mandate for the Modern Church

The Great Commission is not fulfilled by agreement, but by obedience. Every generation must choose whether it will preserve the gospel or proclaim it.

The Church is most faithful not when it is comfortable, but when it is obedient.

Reflection Questions

1. Why is the Great Commission binding on every believer?
2. What lessons from the Book of Acts challenge modern evangelism?
3. How does understanding evangelism as identity change your perspective?

Personal Assignments

- **Assignment 1 — Scripture Study:** Read Matthew 28:18–20 and Acts 1–4. Identify what God promises and what He commands.
- **Assignment 2 — Personal Obedience:** Ask God where He is calling you to be more intentional in witnessing.
- **Assignment 3 — Prayerful Availability:** Pray daily for boldness and obedience, trusting God with results.

Ministry / Small-Group Assignments

Group Discussion

Compare evangelism in Acts with modern church practices. What has changed—and what should not?

Teaching Activity

Create a simple outline of the Great Commission and discuss how each part applies today.

Group Prayer

Pray for renewed obedience, Spirit-empowered boldness, and faithfulness to Christ's mission.

Prayer

Lord Jesus, You have all authority in heaven and on earth, and You have entrusted Your mission to Your Church. Forgive us where we have neglected or minimized Your command. Renew our obedience, strengthen our faith, and empower us by Your Holy Spirit. Teach us to live as witnesses wherever You place us. May we be faithful to proclaim, disciple, and obey—until You return. In Your holy name, Amen.

Chapter 2
Reflection & Notes Worksheet
Equipped to Evangelize

Chapter Title: The Great Commission and the Early Church
Date: _____

Key Scriptures from This Chapter (Write the Bible verses that stood out most to you.)

_____
_____
_____
_____
_____
_____
_____

Main Truths & Key Insights (What were the most important teachings or ideas in this chapter?)

_____
_____
_____
_____
_____
_____
_____

Personal Reflection (How did this chapter challenge, encourage, or correct your thinking?)

_____
_____
_____
_____
_____
_____
_____

Application to My Life (What changes, actions, or attitudes does God want you to apply?)

_____
_____
_____
_____
_____
_____

Evangelism Focus (How does this chapter help you grow as a witness for Christ?)

_____
_____
_____
_____
_____

Prayer Response (Write a prayer in response to what you learned.

_____
_____
_____
_____
_____
_____

Questions I Still Have (Write any questions you want to study further or discuss.)

_____
_____
_____
_____
_____
_____

Action Step for This Week (One practical step you will take based on this chapter.)

_____

_____

_____

_____

_____

_____

_____

Additional Notes

_____

_____

_____

_____

_____

_____

_____

Discussion Notes / Group Insights:

_____

_____

_____

_____

_____

_____

_____

CHAPTER 3
Dependence on the Holy Spirit
Divine Guidance, Conviction, and Power

Evangelism Is Impossible Without the Holy Spirit

True evangelism is not powered by eloquence, personality, or persuasion. It is accomplished through the **active work of the Holy Spirit**. Without Him, evangelism becomes religious speech. With Him, the gospel becomes **living power**.

From the beginning, God made it clear that His redemptive work would never depend on human strength alone:

"Not by might, nor by power, but by my spirit, saith the Lord of hosts." — Zechariah 4:6

Any approach to evangelism that minimizes the Holy Spirit misunderstands both the gospel and the mission.

The Holy Spirit: The True Evangelist

While believers are called to witness, Scripture reveals that the Holy Spirit is the **primary agent of evangelism**. He prepares hearts, opens understanding, and brings conviction.
Jesus Himself declared:

"And when he is come, he will reprove the world of sin, and of righteousness, and of judgment." — John 16:8

Believers do not convince sinners into salvation. They bear witness while the Spirit does the transforming work. This truth relieves pressure and restores confidence.

The Holy Spirit Empowers the Witness

Before the disciples preached publicly, Jesus commanded them to wait:

"But ye shall receive power, after that the Holy Ghost is come upon you: and ye shall be witnesses unto me." — Acts 1:8

Power precedes witness. Boldness follows filling. The early Church did not rely on training manuals alone; it relied on divine empowerment.

This empowerment:
- overcomes fear
- produces boldness
- provides clarity
- sustains endurance

Evangelism becomes effective not when believers feel ready, but when they are **filled and surrendered**.

Guidance and Timing in Evangelism

The Holy Spirit not only empowers evangelism—He **directs it**. Scripture repeatedly shows believers being guided in where to go, when to speak, and whom to approach.

Examples from Acts include:
- Philip being led to the Ethiopian eunuch
- Peter being directed to Cornelius
- Paul being restrained and redirected in missionary journeys

Spirit-led evangelism recognizes that **timing matters**. Speaking too soon or too late can hinder receptivity. Dependence on the Spirit cultivates discernment.

Conviction of the Hearer

One of the most misunderstood aspects of evangelism is conviction. Conviction is not produced by pressure, argument, or emotional manipulation. It is the sovereign work of the Holy Spirit.

The Spirit convicts:

- **of sin** — revealing the need for repentance
- **of righteousness** — pointing to Christ as Savior
- **of judgment** — clarifying eternal realities

Believers are called to speak truth faithfully, trusting the Spirit to apply it personally.

Dependence Over Technique

Techniques may assist communication, but they must never replace dependence. When evangelism becomes method-centered rather than Spirit-centered, it risks manipulation or burnout.

Dependence on the Holy Spirit produces:
- humility instead of pride
- prayer instead of pressure
- obedience instead of control

Faithful evangelism flows from **listening as much as speaking**.

Prayer as the Foundation of Spirit-Led Evangelism

Prayer aligns the evangelist with God's heart and prepares the soil of the hearer's heart. The early Church consistently prayed for boldness, guidance, and open doors.

"Praying always with all prayer and supplication in the Spirit." — Ephesians 6:18

Prayer before evangelism invites God's direction. Prayer during evangelism invites His wisdom. Prayer after evangelism entrusts results to Him.

Avoiding the Errors of Self-Reliance

Self-reliance manifests subtly:
- trusting experience over dependence
- valuing results over obedience
- measuring success by response rather than faithfulness

Scripture reminds believers that God deliberately chooses weakness so that His power is unmistakable.

"That the excellency of the power may be of God, and not of us." — 2 Corinthians 4:7

The Fruit of Spirit-Dependent Evangelism

When evangelism flows from dependence on the Holy Spirit:
- fear loses its grip
- obedience becomes joyful
- results are entrusted to God
- perseverance is sustained

Believers become instruments rather than initiators, servants rather than saviors.

A Call to Surrender and Trust

Dependence on the Holy Spirit is not learned in theory; it is practiced in surrender. Evangelism becomes effective when believers trust God beyond themselves and step forward in obedience.

This dependence prepares the foundation for understanding the gospel message itself, which will be explored in the next chapter.

Reflection Questions

1. Why is the Holy Spirit essential to effective evangelism?
2. How does understanding the Spirit as the true Evangelist reduce fear and pressure?
3. In what ways can prayer deepen dependence on the Holy Spirit?

Personal Assignments

- **Assignment 1 — Scripture Meditation:** Read John 14–16 and Acts 1–4, noting the role of the Holy Spirit in witness.
- **Assignment 2 — Prayer Practice:** Commit to intentional prayer before any evangelistic conversation this week.
- **Assignment 3 — Surrender Reflection:** Ask God to reveal areas where you rely on yourself rather than the Holy Spirit.

Ministry / Small-Group Assignments

Group Discussion

Discuss how churches can shift from program-driven evangelism to Spirit-led obedience.

Teaching Activity

Study examples of Spirit-led guidance in Acts and identify modern parallels.

Group Prayer

Pray together for filling, boldness, discernment, and dependence on the Holy Spirit.

Prayer

Holy Spirit of God, We acknowledge that without You we can do nothing of eternal value. Forgive us for relying on our strength, wisdom, or methods. Fill us afresh with Your power. Guide our steps, open doors, and convict hearts. Teach us to listen, obey, and trust You fully. May every word we speak be empowered by You and bring glory to Jesus Christ. Amen.

Chapter 3
Reflection & Notes Worksheet
Equipped to Evangelize

Chapter Title: Dependence on the Holy Spirit
Date: _____

Key Scriptures from This Chapter (Write the Bible verses that stood out most to you.)

_____

_____

_____

_____

_____

_____

_____

Main Truths & Key Insights (What were the most important teachings or ideas in this chapter?)

_____

_____

_____

_____

_____

_____

_____

Personal Reflection (How did this chapter challenge, encourage, or correct your thinking?)

_____

_____

_____

_____

_____

_____

_____

Application to My Life (What changes, actions, or attitudes does God want you to apply?)

_____
_____
_____
_____
_____
_____

Evangelism Focus (How does this chapter help you grow as a witness for Christ?)

_____
_____
_____
_____
_____

Prayer Response (Write a prayer in response to what you learned.

_____
_____
_____
_____
_____
_____

Questions I Still Have (Write any questions you want to study further or discuss.)

_____
_____
_____
_____
_____
_____

Action Step for This Week (One practical step you will take based on this chapter.)

_____
_____
_____
_____
_____
_____
_____

Additional Notes

_____
_____
_____
_____
_____
_____

Discussion Notes / Group Insights:

_____
_____
_____
_____
_____
_____

CHAPTER 4
¿What Is the Gospel?
Grace, Repentance, Faith, and Salvation

The Central Question of Evangelism

Evangelism ultimately rises or falls on one question: **¿What is the gospel?** If the message is unclear, incomplete, or distorted, the response—no matter how sincere—will rest on a weak foundation.

The gospel is not:
- religious advice
- moral improvement
- cultural Christianity
- self-help spirituality

The gospel is **good news**—a divine announcement of what God has done through Jesus Christ to save sinners.

"Moreover, brethren, I declare unto you the gospel... by which also ye are saved." — 1 Corinthians 15:1–2

The Gospel Is God's Message, Not Ours

The gospel did not originate in human thought. It was revealed by God, accomplished by Christ, and proclaimed by the Church. Evangelists are **stewards**, not inventors, of the message.

Because the gospel belongs to God:
- it must be proclaimed faithfully
- it must not be altered for acceptance
- it must remain Christ-centered
-

Any version of evangelism that shifts the focus away from Christ ceases to be biblical evangelism.

The Problem the Gospel Addresses: Sin

The gospel begins with an honest diagnosis of the human condition. Scripture declares that all humanity stands guilty before a holy God.

"For all have sinned, and come short of the glory of God." — Romans 3:23

Sin is not merely bad behavior; it is rebellion against God that results in separation from Him. Without understanding sin, the gospel loses its meaning. Grace is only good news when the bad news is understood.

Grace: God's Unmerited Favor

At the heart of the gospel stands grace—God's unearned favor toward undeserving sinners.

"For by grace are ye saved through faith; and that not of yourselves: it is the gift of God." — Ephesians 2:8–9

Grace means:

- salvation is initiated by God
- salvation cannot be earned
- salvation is offered freely

Evangelism that minimizes grace turns the gospel into a transaction. Evangelism that magnifies grace points to God's mercy and love.

Repentance: Turning Toward God

Repentance is an essential response to the gospel. It is not merely regret or fear of consequences; it is a **change of mind and direction**—turning away from sin and toward God.

"Repent ye therefore, and be converted, that your sins may be blotted out." — Acts 3:19

True repentance involves:

- acknowledging sin
- turning from self-rule
- surrendering to God's authority

Repentance is not a work that earns salvation; it is the heart's response to grace.

Faith: Trusting in Christ Alone

Faith is how salvation is received. It is not intellectual agreement alone, but personal trust in Jesus Christ as Savior and Lord.

"Believe on the Lord Jesus Christ, and thou shalt be saved." — Acts 16:31

Biblical faith includes:

- belief in who Jesus is
- trust in what He has done
- commitment to follow Him

Faith transfers reliance from self to Christ.

The Person and Work of Jesus Christ

The gospel centers on a Person, not a principle. Jesus Christ is fully God and fully man, sent by the Father to accomplish salvation.

The gospel declares that Jesus:

- lived a sinless life
- died as a substitute for sinners
- rose bodily from the dead
- reigns as Lord

Without Christ, there is no gospel. Without His work, there is no salvation.

Salvation: New Life in Christ

Salvation is more than forgiveness— it is transformation. Those who receive the gospel are:
- forgiven of sin
- reconciled to God
- given new spiritual life
- indwelt by the Holy Spirit

"Therefore if any man be in Christ, he is a new creature." — 2 Corinthians 5:17

Salvation changes identity, direction, and destiny.

The Simplicity and Depth of the Gospel

The gospel is simple enough to be understood by a child, yet profound enough to occupy a lifetime of study. Evangelists must resist the temptation to complicate or dilute it. Clarity is an act of love. **Faithfulness is an act of obedience.**

A Call to Proclaim the Gospel Clearly

The responsibility of the evangelist is not to make the gospel attractive, but to make it **clear**. The Holy Spirit brings conviction and faith.

When the gospel is proclaimed faithfully, God works powerfully.

Reflection Questions

1. Why is clarity about the gospel essential to evangelism?
2. How do grace, repentance, and faith work together in salvation?
3. In what ways can the gospel be unintentionally distorted?

Personal Assignments

- **Assignment 1 — Gospel Summary:** Write a brief explanation of the gospel in your own words, ensuring it includes sin, grace, repentance, faith, and Christ.

- **Assignment 2 — Scripture Study:** Read Romans 3–5 and identify how Paul explains the gospel.

- **Assignment 3 — Prayerful Preparation:** Ask God for opportunities to clearly share the gospel this week.

Ministry / Small-Group Assignments

Group Discussion

Discuss common misunderstandings of the gospel in today's culture.

Teaching Activity

Practice explaining the gospel clearly in two to three minutes.

Group Prayer

Pray for clarity, faithfulness, and confidence in proclaiming the gospel.

Prayer

Gracious Father, Thank You for the good news of salvation through Jesus Christ. Guard our hearts and our words so that we proclaim the gospel clearly and faithfully. Help us never to add to it or subtract from it. Give us wisdom, compassion, and courage as we share the message of grace, repentance, and faith. May many come to know the saving power of Jesus Christ through Your Word proclaimed. Amen.

Chapter 4
Reflection & Notes Worksheet
Equipped to Evangelize

Chapter Title: ¿What Is the Gospel?
Date: _____

Key Scriptures from This Chapter (Write the Bible verses that stood out most to you.)

_____
_____
_____
_____
_____
_____
_____

Main Truths & Key Insights (What were the most important teachings or ideas in this chapter?)

_____
_____
_____
_____
_____
_____
_____

Personal Reflection (How did this chapter challenge, encourage, or correct your thinking?)

_____
_____
_____
_____
_____
_____
_____

Application to My Life (What changes, actions, or attitudes does God want you to apply?)

_____

_____

_____

_____

_____

_____

Evangelism Focus (How does this chapter help you grow as a witness for Christ?)

_____

_____

_____

_____

_____

Prayer Response (Write a prayer in response to what you learned.

_____

_____

_____

_____

_____

_____

Questions I Still Have (Write any questions you want to study further or discuss.)

_____

_____

_____

_____

_____

_____

Action Step for This Week (One practical step you will take based on this chapter.)

_____

_____

_____

_____

_____

_____

_____

Additional Notes

_____

_____

_____

_____

_____

_____

Discussion Notes / Group Insights:

_____

_____

_____

_____

_____

_____

CHAPTER 5
The Cross, the Resurrection, and the True Gospel
The Power and Purity of the Message

The Center of the Christian Message

At the heart of Christianity stands the cross and the empty tomb. Remove either, and the gospel collapses. Evangelism that does not center on the death and resurrection of Jesus Christ may sound spiritual, but it is not the gospel.

The apostle Paul declared:

"For I determined not to know any thing among you, save Jesus Christ, and him crucified." — 1 Corinthians 2:2

The gospel is not an abstract philosophy; it is rooted in historical, redemptive acts accomplished by God through His Son.

The Cross: God's Answer to Sin

The cross reveals both the seriousness of sin and the depth of God's love. Sin demanded judgment; love provided a substitute.

"But God commendeth his love toward us, in that, while we were yet sinners, Christ died for us." — Romans 5:8

On the cross:
- Jesus bore the penalty of sin
- justice was satisfied
- mercy was extended
- reconciliation was made possible

The cross declares that salvation is costly but freely given.

Substitution and Atonement

Jesus did not die as a tragic example or political martyr. He died as a **substitute**.

"Who his own self bare our sins in his own body on the tree." — 1 Peter 2:24

Substitution means:
- Christ took our place
- He bore what we deserved
- He accomplished what we could not

Without substitution, the cross loses its saving power.

The Resurrection: God's Vindication of the Son

If the cross answers the problem of sin, the resurrection answers the problem of death. The resurrection is not optional theology—it is essential.

"If Christ be not risen, then is our preaching vain, and your faith is also vain." — 1 Corinthians 15:14

The resurrection declares that:

- Jesus is truly Lord
- sin has been defeated
- death has been conquered
- salvation is complete

An empty cross without an empty tomb would leave the gospel unfinished.

The Living Christ and Ongoing Power

The resurrection is not merely proof of past victory; it is the source of present power. Jesus is alive and active, interceding for believers and reigning as King.

"Because I live, ye shall live also." — John 14:19
Evangelism proclaims not a memory, but a living Savior.

Guarding the Purity of the Gospel

Because the gospel is powerful, it is often distorted. Scripture repeatedly warns against false or incomplete gospels that remove offense, deny truth, or shift focus from Christ.

Common distortions include:
- a gospel without repentance
- a gospel without the cross
- a gospel without resurrection
- a gospel centered on self rather than Christ

"But though we, or an angel from heaven, preach any other gospel... let him be accursed." — Galatians 1:8

Faithfulness matters more than popularity.

Why a False Gospel Cannot Save

A distorted gospel may attract crowds, but it cannot transform hearts. Only the true gospel carries saving power.

"For I am not ashamed of the gospel of Christ: for it is the power of God unto salvation." — Romans 1:16

When the cross is minimized, grace is misunderstood. When the resurrection is ignored, hope is lost.

Proclaiming Christ Crucified and Risen

Evangelists are not called to soften the message, but to **clarify it**. The offense of the cross is not a flaw—it is the doorway to salvation.

The true gospel:
- humbles the sinner
- exalts the Savior
- offers forgiveness
- demands response

The Power of a Pure Message

When Christ crucified and risen is proclaimed clearly:

- the Holy Spirit convicts
- faith is awakened
- lives are transformed
- God is glorified

The power is not in presentation, but in the message itself.

Reflection Questions

1. Why are both the cross and the resurrection essential to the gospel?
2. What are common ways the gospel is distorted today?
3. How does guarding gospel purity protect both evangelist and hearer?

Personal Assignments

- **Assignment 1 — Scripture Study:** Read 1 Corinthians 15 and Romans 5–8, noting the role of the cross and resurrection.
- **Assignment 2 — Gospel Clarity:** Write a short gospel explanation that clearly includes the cross and the resurrection.
- **Assignment 3 — Prayerful Commitment:** Ask God to guard your heart and words from distorting the gospel.

Ministry / Small-Group Assignments

Group Discussion
- Discuss the difference between a true gospel and a popular but incomplete message.

Teaching Activity
- Compare Paul's preaching in Acts with modern gospel presentations.

Group Prayer
- Pray for faithfulness, courage, and clarity in proclaiming Christ crucified and risen.

Prayer

Heavenly Father, Thank You for the cross where sin was defeated and the empty tomb where death was conquered. Guard our hearts and mouths so that we proclaim the true gospel—pure, powerful, and centered on Jesus Christ. Give us courage to preach Christ crucified and risen, even when it is unpopular. May Your Word accomplish what You desire and bring salvation to many. In Jesus' name, Amen.

Chapter 5
Reflection & Notes Worksheet
Equipped to Evangelize

Chapter Title: The Cross, the Resurrection, and the True Gospel
Date: _____

Key Scriptures from This Chapter (Write the Bible verses that stood out most to you.)

_____
_____
_____
_____
_____
_____
_____

Main Truths & Key Insights (What were the most important teachings or ideas in this chapter?)

_____
_____
_____
_____
_____
_____
_____

Personal Reflection (How did this chapter challenge, encourage, or correct your thinking?)

_____
_____
_____
_____
_____
_____
_____

Application to My Life (What changes, actions, or attitudes does God want you to apply?)

_____
_____
_____
_____
_____
_____

Evangelism Focus (How does this chapter help you grow as a witness for Christ?)

_____
_____
_____
_____
_____

Prayer Response (Write a prayer in response to what you learned.

_____
_____
_____
_____
_____

Questions I Still Have (Write any questions you want to study further or discuss.)

_____
_____
_____
_____
_____
_____

Action Step for This Week (One practical step you will take based on this chapter.)

_____
_____
_____
_____
_____ .
_____
_____

Additional Notes

_____
_____
_____
_____
_____
_____

Discussion Notes / Group Insights:

_____
_____
_____
_____
_____
_____

CHAPTER 6
The Evangelist's Life and Character
Living a Gospel-Worthy Life

The Messenger Matters

While the power of the gospel does not depend on human perfection, the **credibility of the message is deeply affected by the character of the messenger**. Scripture consistently affirms that God uses imperfect people, yet it also calls believers to live lives that align with the truth they proclaim.

The apostle Paul exhorted believers:

"Only let your conversation be as it becometh the gospel of Christ." — Philippians 1:27

Evangelism is not merely about what is said; it is also about **what is seen**. A life shaped by the gospel gives weight to the words that proclaim it.

Grace Before Performance

Living a gospel-worthy life does not mean living a flawless life. Evangelists are not models of perfection, but **testimonies of grace**. Character flows from relationship with Christ, not from external rule-keeping.

Legalism weakens evangelism by producing hypocrisy. Grace strengthens evangelism by producing humility, repentance, and authenticity. The gospel is believable when it is seen transforming real people, not masking them.

Integrity: The Foundation of Credibility

Integrity is consistency between belief and behavior. It does not mean sinless living, but honest living—walking in truth, repentance, and obedience.

"Providing for honest things, not only in the sight of the Lord, but also in the sight of men." — 2 Corinthians 8:21

Integrity:
- builds trust
- removes unnecessary barriers
- protects the witness
- honors Christ

A compromised life may still speak truth, but it often speaks it quietly.

Humility in the Evangelist

Humility guards the evangelist from pride and self-reliance. Evangelism driven by ego points people to the messenger rather than the Savior.

John the Baptist modeled true humility:

"He must increase, but I must decrease." — John 3:30

Humility:
- listens before speaking
- learns from others
- acknowledges weakness
- gives glory to God

God uses humble vessels because they do not compete with His glory.

Love as the Mark of Authentic Witness

Jesus declared that love would be the distinguishing mark of His followers.

"By this shall all men know that ye are my disciples, if ye have love one to another." — John 13:35

Love is not sentimental tolerance; it is sacrificial concern for others' eternal well-being. Evangelism without love sounds harsh. Love without truth becomes incomplete.

True love:

- speaks truth graciously
- shows patience with questions
- responds gently to opposition
- perseveres despite rejection

Love makes the gospel visible.

Holiness Without Hypocrisy

Scripture calls believers to holiness, not to impress others, but to honor God.

"Be ye holy; for I am holy." — 1 Peter 1:16

Holiness is separation **unto** God, not withdrawal **from** people. A holy life does not isolate the evangelist; it distinguishes them. When believers stumble—and they will—repentance restores credibility more powerfully than denial.

Consistency in Public and Private Life

Evangelistic credibility grows when faith is lived consistently across settings—home, work, church, and community.
Inconsistency creates confusion. Consistency invites curiosity.

People are more likely to listen when they see:
- integrity at work
- kindness under pressure
- forgiveness in conflict
- peace in hardship

Daily life becomes a living testimony.

Spiritual Growth Sustains the Witness

Evangelists must continue growing spiritually. Neglect of prayer, Scripture, and fellowship weakens witness over time.

Spiritual disciplines do not earn credibility— they **sustain it**. A growing relationship with Christ keeps the evangelist grounded, teachable, and dependent on God.

Failure, Repentance, and Restoration

Every evangelist will fail at times. Scripture does not hide the failures of God's servants, but it also reveals God's restoring grace.

- Peter denied Christ—and was restored.
- Paul persecuted the Church—and was transformed.

Failure does not end evangelism. **Unrepentance does.**

A Life That Points Beyond Itself

The ultimate purpose of character is not moral display, but **Christ-centered witness**. The evangelist's life should direct attention beyond itself to the Savior.

A gospel-worthy life does not demand admiration—it invites consideration of Christ.

Reflection Questions

1. How does the character of the messenger affect the credibility of the gospel?
2. Why is humility essential to effective evangelism?
3. How can repentance strengthen rather than weaken witness?

Personal Assignments

- **Assignment 1 — Self-Examination:** Ask God to reveal areas of life that may hinder your witness, and commit them to Him in prayer.

- **Assignment 2 — Scripture Study:** Read Philippians 2:1–11 and reflect on Christ's example of humility.

- **Assignment 3 — Intentional Living:** Identify one area this week where you can intentionally reflect Christlike character.

Ministry / Small-Group Assignments

Group Discussion

- Discuss how churches can model gospel integrity without falling into legalism.

Teaching Activity

- Study biblical examples of restored leaders and discuss lessons for evangelism.

Group Prayer

- Pray for integrity, humility, love, and consistency in witness.

Prayer

Heavenly Father, Thank You for Your grace that saves and transforms. Shape our lives so that they reflect the gospel we proclaim. Guard us from pride, hypocrisy, and self-reliance. Teach us to walk in humility, love, and integrity. When we fail, lead us to repentance and restoration. May our lives point clearly to Jesus Christ and bring honor to Your name. Amen.

Chapter 6
Reflection & Notes Worksheet
Equipped to Evangelize

Chapter Title: The Evangelist's Life and Character
Date: _____

Key Scriptures from This Chapter (Write the Bible verses that stood out most to you.)

_____
_____
_____
_____
_____
_____
_____

Main Truths & Key Insights (What were the most important teachings or ideas in this chapter?)

_____
_____
_____
_____
_____
_____
_____

Personal Reflection (How did this chapter challenge, encourage, or correct your thinking?)

_____
_____
_____
_____
_____
_____
_____

Application to My Life (What changes, actions, or attitudes does God want you to apply?)

_____

_____

_____

_____

_____

_____

Evangelism Focus (How does this chapter help you grow as a witness for Christ?)

_____

_____

_____

_____

_____

Prayer Response (Write a prayer in response to what you learned.

_____

_____

_____

_____

_____

Questions I Still Have (Write any questions you want to study further or discuss.)

_____

_____

_____

_____

_____

Action Step for This Week (One practical step you will take based on this chapter.)

_____

_____

_____

_____

_____

_____

_____

Additional Notes

_____

_____

_____

_____

_____

_____

Discussion Notes / Group Insights:

_____

_____

_____

_____

_____

_____

CHAPTER 7
Your Personal Testimony
Sharing What Christ Has Done for You with Compassion and Credibility

The Power of a Transformed Life

God often uses personal testimony as a bridge between gospel truth and the human heart. While Scripture is the ultimate authority, a changed life provides a living demonstration of its power.

Jesus repeatedly affirmed the value of testimony. After delivering a man from demonic bondage, He instructed him:

"Go home to thy friends, and tell them how great things the Lord hath done for thee." — Mark 5:19

A personal testimony does not replace the gospel; it **supports and illustrates it**. It answers the unspoken question many ask: *¿What difference does Christ really make?*

What a Testimony Is—and Is Not

A biblical testimony is not a performance or dramatic retelling designed to impress. It is a truthful account of God's work in a person's life.

A testimony is:
- God-centered, not self-centered
- honest, not exaggerated
- humble, not sensational
- connected to the gospel

A testimony is **not**:
- a sermon
- a debate
- a replacement for Scripture
- a measure of spiritual maturity

God uses both dramatic conversions and quiet transformations.

The Structure of a Clear Testimony

An effective testimony can often be shared in three simple movements:

1. **Life Before Christ**: A brief, honest description of life apart from Christ—without glorifying sin.
2. **How You Came to Christ**: The moment or process through which the gospel became personal—highlighting God's grace.
3. **Life Since Knowing Christ**: The ongoing transformation—new desires, forgiveness, purpose, and hope.

Clarity matters more than length. A testimony should invite conversation, not dominate it.

Keeping the Focus on Christ

The power of testimony lies not in personal experience alone, but in pointing to Christ as Savior and Lord.

A testimony should consistently answer:
- Who saved you?
- Why did you need saving?
- What has Christ changed?

When the focus remains on Christ, the testimony complements the gospel message rather than competing with it.

Compassion: Speaking from Love, Not Superiority

Testimony must be shared with compassion. Evangelism that lacks love often creates resistance rather than openness.

The apostle Paul modeled this posture:

"I tell you even weeping, that they are the enemies of the cross of Christ." — Philippians 3:18

Compassion means:

- listening before speaking
- respecting the person, even when disagreeing
- acknowledging shared brokenness
- speaking truth with gentleness

People are more receptive when they feel understood rather than judged.

Credibility Through Authenticity

Authenticity strengthens credibility. Pretending to have everything together often creates distance rather than trust.

Honest testimony acknowledges:

- ongoing growth
- struggles and dependence on grace
- God's patience and faithfulness

Authenticity invites others to consider Christ without feeling pressured to appear perfect.

Adapting Testimony to the Listener

Wisdom requires sensitivity to context. A testimony shared with a family member may differ from one shared with a coworker or stranger.

Adaptation does not mean compromise. It means:
- choosing language the listener understands
- focusing on shared experiences
- avoiding unnecessary details

The goal is connection, not complexity.

When Testimony Opens the Door to Scripture

A personal testimony often prepares the heart for Scripture. Once interest is sparked, God's Word provides clarity and authority.

Testimony opens the door.
Scripture explains the truth.
The Holy Spirit brings conviction.

Used together, they form a powerful powerful witness.

Avoiding Common Pitfalls

Common mistakes include:
- making testimony too long
- focusing excessively on past sin
- presenting Christianity as problem-free
- using religious jargon

Faithful testimony reflects honesty, hope, and humility.

Every Believer Has a Testimony

Testimony is not reserved for the outspoken or dramatic. Every believer can say, truthfully:

"I once was lost, but now am found."

God delights in using ordinary stories to accomplish extraordinary work.

Reflection Questions

1. Why is personal testimony a powerful tool in evangelism?
2. How can compassion increase the effectiveness of testimony?
3. What elements should always remain central in a testimony?

Personal Assignments

- **Assignment 1 — Write Your Testimony:** Write a short version of your testimony (3–5 minutes) using the three-part structure.
- **Assignment 2 — Prayerful Readiness:** Pray for opportunities to share your testimony naturally this week.
- **Assignment 3 — Scripture Connection:** Identify one Scripture verse that connects clearly to your testimony.

Ministry / Small-Group Assignments

Group Discussion
- Share testimonies within the group and discuss how they point to Christ.

Teaching Activity
- Practice sharing testimonies clearly and compassionately in small groups.

Group Prayer
- Pray for boldness, humility, and love when sharing personal stories of God's grace.

Prayer

Gracious Father, Thank You for the work You have done in our lives through Jesus Christ. Teach us to share our stories with humility, compassion, and truth. Help us point others beyond ourselves to the Savior who transforms hearts. Give us wisdom to speak at the right time and love to listen well. May our testimonies glorify You and draw others to the hope found in Christ alone. Amen.

Chapter 7
Reflection & Notes Worksheet
Equipped to Evangelize

Chapter Title: Your Personal Testimony
Date: _____

Key Scriptures from This Chapter (Write the Bible verses that stood out most to you.)

_____
_____
_____
_____
_____
_____
_____

Main Truths & Key Insights (What were the most important teachings or ideas in this chapter?)

_____
_____
_____
_____
_____
_____
_____

Personal Reflection (How did this chapter challenge, encourage, or correct your thinking?)

_____
_____
_____
_____
_____
_____
_____

Application to My Life (What changes, actions, or attitudes does God want you to apply?)

_____
_____
_____
_____
_____
_____

Evangelism Focus (How does this chapter help you grow as a witness for Christ?)

_____
_____
_____
_____
_____

Prayer Response (Write a prayer in response to what you learned.

_____
_____
_____
_____
_____

Questions I Still Have (Write any questions you want to study further or discuss.)

_____
_____
_____
_____
_____
_____

Action Step for This Week (One practical step you will take based on this chapter.)

_____
_____
_____
_____
_____
_____
_____

Additional Notes

_____
_____
_____
_____
_____
_____

Discussion Notes / Group Insights:

_____
_____
_____
_____
_____
_____

CHAPTER 8
Beginning Gospel Conversations
Opening Doors Naturally and Wisely

Why Starting Is Often the Hardest Part

For many believers, the greatest challenge in evangelism is not understanding the gospel—it is **starting the conversation**. Fear of awkwardness, rejection, or saying the wrong thing often silences sincere hearts.

Yet Scripture shows that evangelism most often begins **relationally**, not formally. Gospel conversations are rarely announced; they are invited through presence, listening, and discernment.

Beginning well matters because a wise opening:
- lowers defenses
- builds trust
- invites dialogue
- prepares the heart for truth

Evangelism is not about forcing conversations, but about **recognizing opportunities God is already creating**.

God Often Opens the Door Before We Speak

Believers are not responsible for creating spiritual interest; God is. Scripture repeatedly shows God arranging encounters and preparing hearts before a word is spoken.

"No man can come to me, except the Father which hath sent me draw him." — John 6:44

Recognizing this truth removes pressure. Evangelists are not salespeople; they are witnesses responding to divine invitations.

The Importance of Listening First

Wise evangelism begins with listening. Listening communicates respect and reveals where a person truly is—spiritually, emotionally, and intellectually.

James exhorts believers:
"Let every man be swift to hear, slow to speak." — James 1:19

Listening helps the evangelist:
- understand the person's worldview
- identify spiritual hunger or resistance
- respond thoughtfully rather than reactively
- avoid unnecessary arguments

People are more open to the gospel when they feel heard.

Everyday Bridges to Gospel Conversations

Gospel conversations often emerge naturally from ordinary topics of life. God frequently uses shared experiences as bridges to spiritual truth.

Common bridges include:

- personal struggles or suffering
- questions about purpose or meaning
- family concerns
- moral or cultural discussions
- expressions of fear, guilt, or hope

Rather than steering abruptly toward religion, the evangelist listens for **openings**—moments when spiritual realities naturally surface.

Asking Thoughtful Questions

Questions invite dialogue and reflection. Jesus frequently used questions to engage hearts and reveal deeper issues.

Examples of gentle, open-ended questions:
- "How do you usually handle difficult seasons in life?"
- "What do you think gives life meaning?"
- "Have you ever thought much about spiritual things?"

Questions should be asked with genuine interest, not as traps. A sincere question often opens the door wider than a prepared speech.

Sharing Faith Naturally

When the opportunity arises, sharing faith should feel **relational, not rehearsed**. The goal is clarity and sincerity, not perfection.

Natural sharing often sounds like:
- "Can I share what has helped me?"
- "My faith has shaped how I see that."
- "I've found hope in Christ during similar moments."

Such statements invite conversation rather than confrontation.

Discernment: Knowing When to Speak and When to Wait

Not every moment is the right moment. The Holy Spirit provides discernment regarding timing and depth.

Scripture reminds believers:
"A word spoken in due season, how good is it!" — Proverbs 15:23

Sometimes faithfulness means planting a seed rather than harvesting immediately. Silence, patience, and prayer can be acts of obedience.

Respect Without Compromise

Beginning gospel conversations requires respect for people without compromising truth. Respect does not mean agreement, and kindness does not mean silence.

Evangelists are called to:
- speak truth graciously
- honor people as image-bearers
- avoid argumentative tones
- remain firm in conviction

A respectful approach keeps the door open for future conversations.

When Conversations Do Not Go Well

Not every conversation will lead to openness. Some may end quickly or awkwardly. Scripture prepares believers for this reality. Faithfulness is measured by obedience, not outcome. Even brief or difficult conversations can plant seeds God later brings to fruit.

The Role of Prayer in Beginning Conversations

Prayer prepares both the evangelist and the hearer. Praying before conversations invites God's guidance; praying after entrusts results to Him.

Prayer helps believers:
- overcome fear
- listen with wisdom
- speak with clarity
- rest in God's sovereignty

Confidence Rooted in God, Not Self

Confidence in evangelism does not come from personality or experience. It comes from trust in God's presence and power.

"For God hath not given us the spirit of fear; but of power, and of love, and of a sound mind." — 2 Timothy 1:7

God delights in using willing, imperfect servants.

Reflection Questions

1. Why do many believers find it difficult to start gospel conversations?
2. How does listening shape more effective evangelism?
3. What everyday situations could become bridges to spiritual conversations?

Personal Assignments

- **Assignment 1 — Awareness Practice:** This week, intentionally listen for moments where spiritual themes naturally arise in conversation.
- **Assignment 2 — Question Preparation:** Write three open-ended questions you could use to invite spiritual dialogue.
- **Assignment 3 — Prayerful Readiness:** Pray daily for sensitivity to the Holy Spirit's prompting to begin conversations.

Ministry / Small-Group Assignments

Group Discussion

- Share examples of how gospel conversations have begun naturally in daily life.

Teaching Activity

- Role-play conversation starters that lead gently toward spiritual topics.

Group Prayer

- Pray for courage, discernment, and wisdom in beginning gospel conversations.

Prayer

Heavenly Father, Thank You for going before us and preparing hearts. Teach us to listen well, speak wisely, and trust You completely. Remove fear and replace it with love and discernment. Help us recognize the opportunities You place before us and to respond with obedience and grace. May every conversation be guided by Your Spirit and used for Your glory. In Jesus' name, Amen.

Chapter 8
Reflection & Notes Worksheet
Equipped to Evangelize

Chapter Title: Beginning Gospel Conversations
Date: _____

Key Scriptures from This Chapter (Write the Bible verses that stood out most to you.)

_____
_____
_____
_____
_____
_____
_____

Main Truths & Key Insights (What were the most important teachings or ideas in this chapter?)

_____
_____
_____
_____
_____
_____
_____

Personal Reflection (How did this chapter challenge, encourage, or correct your thinking?)

_____
_____
_____
_____
_____
_____
_____

Application to My Life (What changes, actions, or attitudes does God want you to apply?)

_____
_____
_____
_____
_____
_____

Evangelism Focus (How does this chapter help you grow as a witness for Christ?)

_____
_____
_____
_____
_____

Prayer Response (Write a prayer in response to what you learned.

_____
_____
_____
_____
_____

Questions I Still Have (Write any questions you want to study further or discuss.)

_____
_____
_____
_____
_____

Action Step for This Week (One practical step you will take based on this chapter.)

_____
_____
_____
_____
_____
_____
_____

Additional Notes

_____
_____
_____
_____
_____
_____

Discussion Notes / Group Insights:

_____
_____
_____
_____
_____
_____

CHAPTER 9
Scripture-Centered and One-on-One Evangelism
Letting God's Word Do the Work

Why Scripture Must Be Central

Evangelism is most effective when it is **anchored in Scripture**. Personal stories, thoughtful reasoning, and sincere compassion all have a place, but none carry the authority or transforming power of God's Word.

"For the word of God is quick, and powerful, and sharper than any two-edged sword." — Hebrews 4:12

When Scripture is central, evangelism shifts from persuasion to proclamation, from human effort to divine action. God's Word reveals truth, confronts the heart, and invites faith.

One-on-One Evangelism in the Ministry of Jesus

Jesus often engaged people personally. He spoke to individuals with care, clarity, and truth— meeting them where they were while guiding them toward repentance and faith.

Examples include:

- Nicodemus, who needed understanding (John 3)
- The Samaritan woman, who needed truth and grace (John 4)
- Zacchaeus, who needed restoration (Luke 19)

In each encounter, Jesus addressed the heart and pointed to God's truth. One-on-one evangelism allows space for questions, honesty, and personal response.

The Role of Scripture in Personal Conversations

Scripture gives evangelism its **content and authority**. While conversation may open the door, God's Word explains the way.

Effective use of Scripture:

- clarifies God's character
- explains humanity's need
- reveals Christ's saving work
- calls for repentance and faith

Believers do not need to quote many verses. A few well-chosen passages, shared clearly and respectfully, allow God's Word to speak.

Letting Scripture Speak for Itself

One common mistake is using Scripture merely to support personal opinions. Faithful evangelism allows Scripture to **stand on its own**.

"So then faith cometh by hearing, and hearing by the word of God." — Romans 10:17

When Scripture is read or explained plainly:

- hearts are confronted with truth
- excuses are challenged
- faith is invited

The Holy Spirit applies the Word personally and powerfully.

Key Scriptures Often Used in Evangelism

While the entire Bible points to Christ, certain passages clearly present the gospel. Examples include:

- Romans 3:23 — the reality of sin
- Romans 6:23 — the consequence of sin and gift of life
- Romans 5:8 — God's love demonstrated
- Acts 16:31 — the call to believe
- Ephesians 2:8–9 — salvation by grace

Knowing these passages equips believers to share the gospel confidently and clearly.

Engaging the Listener with Scripture
One-on-one evangelism is dialogical, not monological. Scripture can be introduced through questions such as:
- "May I share a verse that has helped me?"
- "What do you think this passage means?"

Inviting the listener to read or respond encourages engagement rather than resistance.

Clarity Without Overload

Clarity is more important than quantity. Overloading a conversation with verses can overwhelm rather than enlighten.

Effective Scripture-centered evangelism:
- focuses on key truths
- explains verses simply
- avoids unnecessary jargon
- allows time for reflection

The goal is understanding, not impressing.

Handling Questions While Staying Scripture-Focused

Questions are opportunities, not interruptions. When questions arise, Scripture provides a trustworthy anchor.

When unsure of an answer:

- acknowledge limits honestly
- return to what Scripture clearly teaches
- commit to follow up if needed

Humility builds trust and keeps the focus on God's Word.

Trusting God with the Outcome

One-on-one evangelism requires patience. Not every conversation ends with immediate response. Scripture often works over time, producing fruit unseen by the evangelist.

"I have planted, Apollos watered; but God gave the increase." — 1 Corinthians 3:6

Faithfulness involves planting seeds and trusting God for growth.

The Power of Scripture Combined with Relationship

When Scripture is shared within a caring relationship, its impact is often deeper. Truth spoken in love invites consideration rather than defensiveness.

Scripture-centered evangelism respects the person while honoring God's truth.

Reflection Questions
1. Why is Scripture essential to effective evangelism?
2. How does one-on-one evangelism differ from public proclamation?
3. What Scriptures are you most comfortable sharing, and why?

Personal Assignments
- **Assignment 1 — Scripture Familiarity:** Choose five gospel-centered verses and memorize or study them for clarity.
- **Assignment 2 — Practice Conversation:** Practice explaining one Scripture passage clearly in your own words.
- **Assignment 3 — Prayerful Trust:** Pray for patience and trust as you share God's Word with others.

Ministry / Small-Group Assignments

- **Group Discussion:** Discuss how Scripture can remain central without making conversations feel forced.
- **Teaching Activity:** Role-play one-on-one evangelism scenarios using Scripture naturally.
- **Group Prayer:** Pray for confidence in God's Word and sensitivity to the Holy Spirit.

Prayer
Heavenly Father, Thank You for the living and powerful Word You have given us. Teach us to trust its authority and depend on Your Spirit to apply it to hearts. Give us wisdom to share Scripture clearly and lovingly. Help us remain faithful in planting seeds and patient in waiting for Your work. May Your Word accomplish all that You desire and draw many to saving faith in Jesus Christ. Amen.

Chapter 9
Reflection & Notes Worksheet
Equipped to Evangelize

Chapter Title: Scripture-Centered and One-on-One Evangelism
Date: _____

Key Scriptures from This Chapter (Write the Bible verses that stood out most to you.)

_____
_____
_____
_____
_____
_____
_____

Main Truths & Key Insights (What were the most important teachings or ideas in this chapter?)

_____
_____
_____
_____
_____
_____
_____

Personal Reflection (How did this chapter challenge, encourage, or correct your thinking?)

_____
_____
_____
_____
_____
_____
_____

Application to My Life (What changes, actions, or attitudes does God want you to apply?)

_____
_____
_____
_____
_____
_____

Evangelism Focus (How does this chapter help you grow as a witness for Christ?)

_____
_____
_____
_____
_____

Prayer Response (Write a prayer in response to what you learned.

_____
_____
_____
_____
_____
_____

Questions I Still Have (Write any questions you want to study further or discuss.)

_____
_____
_____
_____
_____

Action Step for This Week (One practical step you will take based on this chapter.)

_____
_____
_____
_____
_____
_____
_____

Additional Notes

_____
_____
_____
_____
_____
_____
_____

Discussion Notes / Group Insights:

_____
_____
_____
_____
_____
_____
_____

CHAPTER 10

Inviting a Response
Repentance, Faith, and Decision

Why an Invitation Matters

Evangelism does not end with explanation alone. The gospel is a message that **calls for response**. While believers cannot compel a decision, they are called to present the truth clearly and invite hearers to respond to God's grace.

Scripture consistently connects proclamation with invitation:
"Now then we are ambassadors for Christ... we pray you in Christ's stead, be ye reconciled to God." — 2 Corinthians 5:20

An invitation honors the listener's responsibility before God and clarifies what the gospel asks of the heart.

The Nature of a Biblical Response

A biblical response to the gospel is not merely emotional agreement or intellectual acknowledgment. Scripture presents response in terms of **repentance and faith**—a turning from sin and a trusting surrender to Jesus Christ.

"Repent ye, and believe the gospel." — Mark 1:15

This response involves:
- recognizing one's need before God
- turning away from self-rule and sin
- trusting in Christ alone for salvation

Inviting a response means making these realities clear, not rushing the hearer.

Clarity Without Coercion

One of the greatest dangers in evangelism is confusing clarity with pressure. Coercion may produce outward compliance, but it does not produce genuine faith.

Biblical invitations:

- explain what God calls for
- allow space for reflection
- respect the work of the Holy Spirit
- avoid emotional manipulation

Jesus Himself often invited response without forcing it. Some followed immediately; others walked away. Faithfulness does not require controlling outcomes.

Recognizing Readiness

Not every hearer is ready to respond immediately. Discernment—guided by the Holy Spirit— helps the evangelist recognize openness, hesitation, or resistance.

Signs of readiness may include:

- sincere questions about salvation
- awareness of sin or need
- desire for prayer
- interest in Scripture

When readiness is evident, loving clarity becomes an act of care.

How to Invite a Response Wisely

Invitations should be simple, clear, and respectful. Examples include:

- "Would you like to place your trust in Christ today?"
- "Do you feel ready to turn to God and receive His forgiveness?"
- "Can I help you pray and respond to what God is showing you?"

The goal is not to script a moment, but to **guide a sincere response**.

The Role of Prayer in Response

Prayer often accompanies a response to the gospel, but prayer itself does not save. Salvation rests in faith in Christ, not in repeating words.

Prayer:
- expresses repentance and trust
- invites God's grace
- marks a moment of surrender

Evangelists should explain that prayer reflects faith—it does not replace it.

When the Answer Is "Not Yet"

Some hearers need time. Scripture shows that faith often grows gradually.

A respectful response to hesitation includes:

- affirming the seriousness of the decision
- encouraging continued reflection
- offering Scripture for further reading
- committing to prayer

Patience preserves relationship and honors God's timing.

Avoiding False Assurance

False assurance harms souls. Evangelists must avoid equating salvation with raised hands, repeated prayers, or momentary emotion.

True assurance is rooted in:
- repentance toward God
- faith in Jesus Christ
- the promises of Scripture

Clarity protects both the hearer and the witness.

Entrusting the Outcome to God

Inviting a response is an act of obedience; conversion is an act of God. Evangelists must resist measuring success by immediate decisions.

"The Lord opened her heart, that she attended unto the things which were spoken of Paul." — Acts 16:14

God alone opens hearts. Faithfulness invites response and trusts Him with results.

Reflection Questions

1. Why is inviting a response an essential part of evangelism?
2. How can clarity be maintained without pressure or manipulation?
3. What dangers arise when false assurance is given?

Personal Assignments

- **Assignment 1 — Gospel Invitation Practice:** Write a clear, respectful invitation you could use in a gospel conversation.
- **Assignment 2 — Scripture Study:** Read Acts 2, Acts 16, and Romans 10. Identify how response is presented in Scripture.
- **Assignment 3 — Prayerful Dependence:** Ask God for wisdom to recognize readiness and patience to respect His timing.

Ministry / Small-Group Assignments

- **Group Discussion:** Discuss how churches can invite response while avoiding emotional manipulation.
- **Teaching Activity:** Role-play gospel conversations that end with a respectful invitation.
- **Group Prayer:** Pray for discernment, courage, and faithfulness when inviting response.

Prayer

Heavenly Father, Thank You for calling us to proclaim the gospel with clarity and love. Give us wisdom to invite response without pressure and courage to speak truth faithfully. Teach us to trust Your Spirit to convict hearts and lead people to repentance and faith. Guard us from manipulation and false assurance, and help us honor You in every invitation we extend. In Jesus' name, Amen.

Chapter 10
Reflection & Notes Worksheet
Equipped to Evangelize

Chapter Title: Inviting a Response
Date: _____

Key Scriptures from This Chapter (Write the Bible verses that stood out most to you.)

_____
_____
_____
_____
_____
_____
_____

Main Truths & Key Insights (What were the most important teachings or ideas in this chapter?)

_____
_____
_____
_____
_____
_____
_____

Personal Reflection (How did this chapter challenge, encourage, or correct your thinking?)

_____
_____
_____
_____
_____
_____
_____

Application to My Life (What changes, actions, or attitudes does God want you to apply?)

_____

_____

_____

_____

_____

_____

Evangelism Focus (How does this chapter help you grow as a witness for Christ?)

_____

_____

_____

_____

_____

Prayer Response (Write a prayer in response to what you learned.

_____

_____

_____

_____

_____

_____

Questions I Still Have (Write any questions you want to study further or discuss.)

_____

_____

_____

_____

_____

Action Step for This Week (One practical step you will take based on this chapter.)

_____
_____
_____
_____
_____
_____
_____

Additional Notes

_____
_____
_____
_____
_____
_____

Discussion Notes / Group Insights:

_____
_____
_____
_____
_____
_____

CHAPTER 11

Evangelism in Daily Relationships
Home, Workplace, School, and Community

Evangelism Where Life Actually Happens

Most evangelism does not occur on platforms or in organized events. It happens in kitchens, classrooms, offices, neighborhoods, and everyday conversations. God has intentionally placed believers within relationships and routines where the gospel can be seen, heard, and lived.

"And how shall they hear without a preacher?" — Romans 10:14

Every believer is already positioned in a mission field. The question is not *where* evangelism should occur, but *how faithfully* believers live and speak where God has placed them.

The Home: The First Mission Field

Scripture consistently presents the home as the primary context for spiritual influence. Faith is meant to be modeled and spoken within close relationships.

"Train up a child in the way he should go..." — Proverbs 22:6

Evangelism in the home includes:

- modeling genuine faith
- speaking truth with patience
- answering questions honestly
- demonstrating forgiveness and grace

In families, credibility is tested daily. Consistence matters. Hypocrisy hinders witness; humility strengthens it.

Reaching Family Members with Wisdom

Evangelizing family requires sensitivity. Familiarity can produce resistance, but love builds bridges.

Wise approaches include:

- prayer before persuasion
- listening more than lecturing
- living faithfully over time
- trusting God with timing

Jesus acknowledged the difficulty of family witness, yet Scripture affirms that God works powerfully within households.

The Workplace: Faith with Integrity

The workplace is a significant mission field where character often speaks louder than words. Scripture calls believers to excellence, honesty, and respect.

"Whatsoever ye do, do it heartily, as to the Lord." — Colossians 3:23

Faithful workplace evangelism includes:

- integrity in responsibilities
- kindness under pressure
- respect for authority
- appropriate, respectful conversation

Evangelism at work is not coercive or disruptive. It is relational, ethical, and grounded in excellence.

Wisdom and Boundaries at Work

Legal and professional boundaries must be honored. Wisdom discerns when to speak openly and when to wait.

Appropriate witnesses often occur:
- during breaks or personal conversations
- when asked about beliefs
- through compassion during crises

Trust built through consistent character often opens doors for meaningful dialogue.

Schools and Academic Environments

Students and educators alike face environments where beliefs are questioned and values are shaped. Evangelism in academic settings requires clarity, courage, and respect.

Faithful witness includes:
- living consistently
- engaging thoughtfully
- answering questions graciously
- refusing compromise without hostility

Young believers especially need encouragement to stand firm without arrogance or fear.

The Community: Presence and Engagement

Communities reflect shared life—celebrations, needs, struggles, and service. Evangelism in the community often begins with **presence**.

"Let your light so shine before men." — Matthew 5:16

Community evangelism includes:

- serving real needs
- building relationships
- demonstrating compassion
- speaking truth when opportunities arise

Acts of kindness do not replace the gospel, but they often prepare hearts to hear it.

Avoiding Two Common Errors

Evangelism in daily life must avoid two extremes:

1. **Silence without Witness**: Living kindly but never speaking truth leaves the gospel unheard.
2. **Words without Relationship**: Speaking abruptly without care often closes hearts.

Biblical evangelism unites **presence and proclamation**.

Faithfulness Over Visibility

Not all evangelism produces visible results. Many seeds are planted quietly and grow unseen.

"Be not weary in well doing: for in due season we shall reap." — Galatians 6:9

God values faithfulness over recognition. Everyday obedience honors Him deeply.

A Life Lived on Mission

Evangelism becomes natural when believers view daily life as sacred opportunity rather than interruption. God works through ordinary faithfulness.

Living sent every day transforms routine into mission.

Reflection Questions

1. Why are daily relationships central to evangelism?
2. What challenges arise when evangelizing in familiar settings?
3. How can wisdom and boldness be held together in daily life?

Personal Assignments

- **Assignment 1 — Relationship Mapping:** Identify key relationships in your life where God may be inviting faithful witness.
- **Assignment 2 — Prayerful Presence:** Commit to praying daily for one setting where you spend significant time.
- **Assignment 3 — Faithful Action:** Look for one tangible way to reflect Christ's love this week.

Ministry / Small-Group Assignments

Group Discussion
- Share experiences of evangelism in daily relationships and lessons learned.

Teaching Activity
- Discuss practical boundaries and opportunities in workplaces and schools.

Group Prayer
- Pray for discernment, courage, and consistency in daily witness.

Prayer

Heavenly Father, Thank You for placing us where we are. Help us see our homes, workplaces, schools, and communities as mission fields You have entrusted to us. Teach us to live faithfully, speak wisely, and love genuinely. Give us patience to trust Your timing and courage to speak when You open doors. May our daily lives reflect the gospel of Jesus Christ and bring glory to Your name. Amen.

Chapter 11
Reflection & Notes Worksheet
Equipped to Evangelize

Chapter Title: Evangelism in Daily Relationships
Date: _____

Key Scriptures from This Chapter (Write the Bible verses that
stood out most to you.)

_____
_____
_____
_____
_____
_____
_____

Main Truths & Key Insights (What were the most important
teachings or ideas in this chapter?)

_____
_____
_____
_____
_____
_____

Personal Reflection (How did this chapter challenge, encourage,
or correct your thinking?)

_____
_____
_____
_____
_____
_____

Application to My Life (What changes, actions, or attitudes does God want you to apply?)

_____
_____
_____
_____
_____
_____

Evangelism Focus (How does this chapter help you grow as a witness for Christ?)

_____
_____
_____
_____
_____

Prayer Response (Write a prayer in response to what you learned.

_____
_____
_____
_____
_____
_____

Questions I Still Have (Write any questions you want to study further or discuss.)

_____
_____
_____
_____
_____
_____

Action Step for This Week (One practical step you will take based on this chapter.)

_____
_____
_____
_____
_____
_____
_____

Additional Notes

_____
_____
_____
_____
_____
_____
_____

Discussion Notes / Group Insights:

_____
_____
_____
_____
_____
_____
_____

CHAPTER 12

Evangelizing in the Digital World
Using Media and Technology for the Gospel

The Mission Field Has Expanded

The digital world has reshaped how people communicate, form relationships, and explore beliefs. Conversations that once happened in homes and marketplaces now occur through screens and platforms. This shift does not change the gospel, but it does expand the places where it can be shared.

"Their line is gone out through all the earth, and their words to the end of the world." — Romans 10:18

Technology is not the mission, but it has become a **mission field**. Faithful evangelism recognizes this reality and engages it wisely.

Biblical Foundations for Digital Witness

Scripture does not name modern technologies, yet it consistently affirms using available means to proclaim God's truth. The early Church used roads, letters, public gatherings, and household networks to spread the gospel.

The method adapted; the message remained the same.

The apostle Paul wrote letters that traveled farther than he could. Today, digital media functions similarly— carrying truth beyond physical limitations.

Biblical principles that guide digital evangelism include:
- faithfulness to truth
- love for people
- clarity of message
- integrity of character

Technology must serve these principles, not replace them.

The Opportunities of Digital Evangelism

Digital platforms offer unprecedented reach and accessibility. Through social media, messaging, video, and online communities, believers can:

- share Scripture widely
- tell testimonies instantly
- engage seekers anonymously
- encourage believers globally

For many, digital spaces feel safer for asking spiritual questions. Evangelism online often becomes a **first step**, not the final one.

The Limits and Dangers of the Digital World

While technology creates opportunity, it also carries limitations. Digital communication can lack tone, context, and relational depth. Misunderstandings spread quickly, and truth competes with misinformation.

Common dangers include:
- reducing the gospel to slogans
- prioritizing popularity over faithfulness
- engaging in argumentative or hostile exchanges
- confusing visibility with effectiveness

Digital evangelism must resist the temptation to value engagement metrics over spiritual fruit.

Truth and Compassion Must Remain United

One of the greatest risks in digital witness is separating truth from compassion. Social platforms can encourage harshness, sarcasm, and public shaming.

Scripture calls believers to a different standard:

"Speaking the truth in love." — Ephesians 4:15

Compassion guards tone. Truth guards content. Both are essential. Evangelism online should reflect the character of Christ as much as the message of Christ.

Using Personal Presence Wisely Online

Believers represent Christ not only in what they post, but in how they interact. Digital presence is a form of public witness.

Wisdom includes:
- posting with integrity
- responding with gentleness
- avoiding unnecessary controversy
- knowing when silence is appropriate

Online behavior can either invite conversation or close doors.

Sharing the Gospel Clearly in Digital Spaces

Clarity matters even more online, where attention spans are short. Faithful digital evangelism:
- points consistently to Christ
- avoids vague spirituality
- includes Scripture appropriately
- invites further conversation

Short content can still be faithful when it directs people toward the full gospel rather than replacing it.

Digital Evangelism as a Bridge, Not a Substitute

Technology can open doors, but it cannot replace embodied discipleship and community. Digital evangelism is often **introductory**, leading toward deeper relationships, church connection, and ongoing discipleship.

Wise digital witness:

- invites questions
- encourages local church involvement
- points beyond the screen
- supports follow-up

The goal is not online followers but transformed lives.

Discernment and Dependence on the Holy Spirit

Digital evangelism still requires spiritual discernment. Timing, tone, and response should be guided by the Holy Spirit, just as in face-to-face witness.

Prayer remains essential:

- before posting
- before responding
- before engaging sensitive topics

The Spirit convicts hearts—online and offline.

Faithfulness in a Fast-Moving World

Digital spaces reward speed, but faithfulness often requires patience. Not every comment must be answered. Not every debate must be joined.

Evangelists are called to plant seeds, not control outcomes. God works beyond what is seen.

Reflection Questions

1. What opportunities does the digital world create for evangelism?
2. What dangers must believers guard against when sharing faith online?
3. How can truth and compassion remain united in digital witness?

Personal Assignments

- **Assignment 1 — Digital Audit:** Review your online presence. Does it reflect Christ's character and truth?
- **Assignment 2 — Intentional Sharing:** Prayerfully share a Scripture, testimony, or gospel-centered message this week.
- **Assignment 3 — Prayer Commitment:** Commit to praying before engaging in spiritual conversations online.

Ministry / Small-Group Assignments

Group Discussion
- Discuss how churches can use digital platforms wisely without compromising discipleship.

Teaching Activity
- Develop guidelines for respectful, Christ-centered online engagement.

Group Prayer
- Pray for wisdom, discernment, and integrity in digital evangelism.

Prayer

Heavenly Father, Thank You for the opportunities You have given us to share Your truth through modern means. Grant us wisdom to use technology faithfully, humility to remain teachable, and love to reflect Your heart. Guard us from pride, distraction, and compromise. May every word we share online honor You and point others to the saving grace of Jesus Christ. Amen.

Chapter 12
Reflection & Notes Worksheet
Equipped to Evangelize

Chapter Title: Evangelizing in the Digital World
Date: _____

Key Scriptures from This Chapter (Write the Bible verses that stood out most to you.)

_____
_____
_____
_____
_____
_____
_____

Main Truths & Key Insights (What were the most important teachings or ideas in this chapter?)

_____
_____
_____
_____
_____
_____
_____

Personal Reflection (How did this chapter challenge, encourage, or correct your thinking?)

_____
_____
_____
_____
_____
_____
_____

Application to My Life (What changes, actions, or attitudes does God want you to apply?)

_____

_____

_____

_____

_____

_____

Evangelism Focus (How does this chapter help you grow as a witness for Christ?)

_____

_____

_____

_____

_____

Prayer Response (Write a prayer in response to what you learned.

_____

_____

_____

_____

_____

Questions I Still Have (Write any questions you want to study further or discuss.)

_____

_____

_____

_____

_____

Action Step for This Week (One practical step you will take based on this chapter.)

_____
_____
_____
_____
_____
_____
_____

Additional Notes

_____
_____
_____
_____
_____
_____

Discussion Notes / Group Insights:

_____
_____
_____
_____
_____
_____

CHAPTER 13

Overcoming Fear, Objections, and Opposition
Standing Firm with Wisdom and Grace

The Reality of Resistance

Wherever the gospel is proclaimed, resistance will follow. Scripture never promises that evangelism will be comfortable, universally welcomed, or free from difficulty. Instead, it prepares believers to expect opposition and to respond with faith, wisdom, and perseverance.

"Yea, and all that will live godly in Christ Jesus shall suffer persecution." — 2 Timothy 3:12

Resistance does not indicate failure. Often, it confirms that the message is being proclaimed faithfully.

Understanding Fear in Evangelism

Fear is one of the greatest internal barriers to evangelism. It may appear as fear of rejection, fear of conflict, fear of inadequacy, or fear of misunderstanding.

Fear thrives when believers:
- focus on themselves rather than Christ
- overestimate human response
- underestimate God's presence

Scripture addresses fear directly:

"For God hath not given us the spirit of fear; but of power, and of love, and of a sound mind." — 2 Timothy 1:7

Fear is not conquered by confidence in self, but by trust in God.

Courage Rooted in God's Presence

Biblical courage is not the absence of fear; it is obedience in spite of it. God repeatedly reassures His people of His presence before sending them into difficult missions.

"Fear thou not; for I am with thee." — Isaiah 41:10

Evangelistic courage grows when believers remember:
- God is present
- God is sovereign
- God is faithful

Confidence rests in who God is, not in how people respond.

Responding to Questions and Objections

Questions and objections are not enemies of faith. Often, they reflect genuine curiosity, confusion, or internal struggle.

Peter exhorts believers:

"Be ready always to give an answer to every man that asketh you a reason of the hope that is in you with meekness and fear." — 1 Peter 3:15

Wise responses:

- listen carefully
- answer honestly
- avoid unnecessary arguments
- remain anchored in Scripture

It is acceptable to admit when an answer is unknown and to commit to further study.

Common Questions and Objections in Evangelism

With Biblical Responses

Evangelism often brings sincere questions, doubts, and objections. These questions should not intimidate believers; they are frequently **doorways to deeper understanding**. Scripture provides clear, gracious answers that point people to Christ rather than to human reasoning.

The goal is not to win arguments, but to **speak truth with grace** and trust the Holy Spirit to work in the heart.

1. "Why does God allow suffering and evil?"

This is one of the most common and emotionally driven questions. It often arises from pain, loss, or injustice rather than intellectual debate.

Biblical Truth

- God did not create evil; sin entered the world through human rebellion
- God is present in suffering and works redemption through it
- Ultimate justice and restoration are promised

Key Scriptures

- Genesis 3:1–19 – The entrance of sin into the world
- Romans 8:18–28 – God working through suffering
- Psalm 34:19 – God's nearness in affliction
- Revelation 21:4 – God's final restoration

2. "Aren't all religions basically the same?"

This question reflects cultural pluralism rather than biblical teaching.

Biblical Truth

- Jesus claimed exclusivity, not arrogance
- Salvation is found in a Person, not a philosophy
- Truth cannot be contradictory

Key Scriptures

- John 14:6 – Jesus as the only way
- Acts 4:12 – Salvation in no other name
- 1 Timothy 2:5 – One mediator between God and man

3. "I'm a good person—why do I need salvation?"

This question assumes morality equals righteousness before God.

Biblical Truth

- God's standard is holiness, not comparison
- Good works cannot erase sin
- Salvation is by grace, not merit

Key Scriptures

- Romans 3:10–23 – No one righteous
- Isaiah 64:6 – Human righteousness insufficient
- Ephesians 2:8–9 – Salvation by grace

4. "How can a loving God send people to hell?"

This question often misunderstands both love and justice.

Biblical Truth

- God does not desire anyone to perish
- Judgment is the result of rejected grace
- Love does not eliminate justice

Key Scriptures

- 2 Peter 3:9 – God's desire for repentance
- John 3:16–19 – Condemnation tied to rejection of light
- Romans 6:23 – Consequence of sin

5. "What about people who never heard about Jesus?"

This question expresses concern for fairness and justice.

Biblical Truth

- God is perfectly just and merciful
- God reveals Himself through creation and conscience
- The question increases urgency for evangelism

Key Scriptures

- Romans 1:18–20 – God revealed through creation
- Romans 2:14–16 – God's justice and conscience
- Genesis 18:25 – God always does what is right

6. "The Bible was written by men—how can it be trusted?"

This question addresses authority and reliability.

Biblical Truth

- Scripture is inspired by God
- God used human authors without error in truth
- Scripture confirms itself through history and prophecy

Key Scriptures

- 2 Timothy 3:16 – Scripture inspired by God
- 2 Peter 1:20–21 – Men moved by the Holy Spirit
- Psalm 119:160 – God's Word is truth

7. "Christians are hypocrites."

This objection often comes from personal hurt or disappointment.

Biblical Truth

- Christianity is about Christ, not human perfection
- Hypocrisy is condemned by Jesus Himself
- Grace transforms imperfect people

Key Scriptures

- Romans 3:23 – All have sinned
- Matthew 23 – Jesus condemns hypocrisy
- 2 Corinthians 5:17 – New life in Christ

8. "If God is good, why does He judge sin?"

This question separates goodness from holiness.

Biblical Truth

- God's goodness includes justice
- Love without justice is not loving
- Judgment protects what is good

Key Scriptures

- Habakkuk 1:13 – God's holiness
- Romans 2:5–6 – God's righteous judgment
- Psalm 89:14 – Justice and righteousness as God's foundation

9. "I don't feel ready to change my life."

This question reflects fear of surrender.

Biblical Truth

- Salvation precedes transformation
- God provides grace for change
- Growth is a process

Key Scriptures

- Matthew 11:28–30 – Come as you are
- 2 Corinthians 5:17 – New creation
- Philippians 1:6 – God completes His work

10. "Why do Christians evangelize so much?"

This question touches motivation and intent.

Biblical Truth

- Evangelism flows from love, not pressure
- God desires all to hear the gospel
- Sharing faith is an act of compassion

Key Scriptures

- Matthew 28:19–20 – The Great Commission
- Romans 10:13–15 – The necessity of sharing
- 2 Corinthians 5:14 – Love of Christ compels us

A Pastoral Reminder for Evangelizers

- You do not need to answer everything perfectly
- Scripture carries more authority than opinions
- Listening matters as much as speaking
- The Holy Spirit convicts and convinces

Faithful evangelism is measured by **obedience**, not by debate victories.

Distinguishing Objections from Resistance

Not every objection is a barrier. Some are invitations to deeper conversation.

Healthy discernment helps distinguish between:

- sincere questions
- emotional resistance
- intellectual barriers
- spiritual struggle

The goal is not to win arguments, but to bear faithful witness.

Rejection: A Common Experience

Rejection is not a sign of unfaithfulness. Even Jesus was rejected by many who heard Him.

"He came unto his own, and his own received him not." — John 1:11

Believers must learn to separate personal worth from gospel response. Rejection is often directed at the message, not the messenger.

Responding well to rejection preserves integrity and keeps doors open for future witness.

Persecution and Opposition in Scripture

The early Church faced hostility, imprisonment, and persecution—yet continued to proclaim the gospel.

"And they departed... rejoicing that they were counted worthy to suffer shame for his name."
— Acts 5:41

Opposition did not silence the Church; it strengthened it. Faithfulness mattered more than safety.

Spiritual Warfare and Evangelism

Scripture reveals that evangelism involves spiritual conflict. The resistance encountered is not merely human.

"For we wrestle not against flesh and blood." — Ephesians 6:12

Spiritual warfare reminds believers:

- people are not the enemy
- deception blinds hearts
- prayer is essential
- God's power is greater

Understanding spiritual warfare prevents bitterness and sustains compassion.

Standing Firm Without Becoming Harsh

Firmness in truth must never become harshness in tone. Scripture consistently calls believers to gentleness, patience, and love—even in opposition.

"The servant of the Lord must not strive; but be gentle unto all men." — 2 Timothy 2:24

Standing firm means refusing compromise while maintaining Christlike character.

Perseverance in Faithful Witness

Evangelism is often a long journey. Seeds planted today may bear fruit years later.

"Let us not be weary in well doing: for in due season we shall reap, if we faint not." — Galatians 6:9

God values perseverance. Faithfulness honors Him regardless of visible results.

Hope That Sustains the Witness

Hope anchors evangelism. Believers trust that God is at work beyond what they see.

"My word... shall not return unto me void." — Isaiah 55:11

This hope sustains courage, patience, and joy—even in difficult seasons.

Reflection Questions

1. What fears most commonly hinder evangelism?
2. How can objections become opportunities for witness?
3. Why is understanding spiritual warfare important in evangelism?

Personal Assignments

- **Assignment 1 — Fear Identification:** Identify specific fears that hinder your witness and commit them to God in prayer.
- **Assignment 2 — Scripture Study:** Read Ephesians 6:10–18 and reflect on God's provision for spiritual strength.
- **Assignment 3 — Courage Practice:** Step intentionally into one gospel conversation this week, trusting God with the outcome.

Ministry / Small-Group Assignments

Group Discussion

- Share experiences of rejection or opposition and discuss how God used them for growth.

Teaching Activity

- Practice responding to common objections with gentleness and Scripture.

Group Prayer

- Pray for boldness, perseverance, and spiritual protection in evangelism.

Prayer

Heavenly Father, We thank You that You have not left us alone in the mission You have given. Strengthen our hearts when fear rises, guide our words when questions come, and sustain us when opposition appears. Teach us to stand firm in truth with humility and love. Clothe us with spiritual strength, protect our hearts from discouragement, and help us persevere faithfully for Your glory. In Jesus' name, Amen.

Chapter 13
Reflection & Notes Worksheet
Equipped to Evangelize

Chapter Title: Overcoming Fear, Objections, and Opposition
Date: _____

Key Scriptures from This Chapter (Write the Bible verses that stood out most to you.)

_____
_____
_____
_____
_____
_____
_____

Main Truths & Key Insights (What were the most important teachings or ideas in this chapter?)

_____
_____
_____
_____
_____
_____
_____

Personal Reflection (How did this chapter challenge, encourage, or correct your thinking?)

_____
_____
_____
_____
_____
_____
_____

Application to My Life (What changes, actions, or attitudes does God want you to apply?)

_____
_____
_____
_____
_____
_____

Evangelism Focus (How does this chapter help you grow as a witness for Christ?)

_____
_____
_____
_____
_____

Prayer Response (Write a prayer in response to what you learned.

_____
_____
_____
_____
_____
_____

Questions I Still Have (Write any questions you want to study further or discuss.)

_____
_____
_____
_____
_____
_____

Action Step for This Week (One practical step you will take based on this chapter.)

_____

_____

_____

_____

_____

_____

_____

Additional Notes

_____

_____

_____

_____

_____

_____

Discussion Notes / Group Insights:

_____

_____

_____

_____

_____

_____

CHAPTER 14

The Moment After Salvation
Caring for New Believers

Salvation Is the Beginning, Not the End

The moment a person responds to the gospel in repentance and faith is a miracle of grace. Sin is forgiven, reconciliation with God is established, and new life begins in Christ. Yet Scripture never treats conversion as the finish line. It marks the **beginning of a lifelong journey**.

"As newborn babes, desire the sincere milk of the word, that ye may grow thereby." — 1 Peter 2:2

Evangelism that ends at decision leaves believers vulnerable and unsupported. Care for new believers is not optional; it is a **biblical responsibility** entrusted to the Church.

The Spiritual Condition of New Believers

New believers are fully saved and fully accepted by God, yet they are spiritually young. Scripture uses the imagery of infancy not to diminish their salvation, but to emphasize their need for nourishment, protection, and guidance.

Healthy care avoids two extremes:

- **Expecting instant maturity**
- **Withholding responsibility and growth**

Patient instruction, encouragement, and clarity help new believers learn to walk in faith with confidence.

Assurance of Salvation: Anchoring Faith in Truth
One of the most immediate needs after salvation is assurance. Feelings fluctuate, doubts arise, and old patterns may still exert influence. Assurance must be grounded not in emotion, but in **God's promises**.

"These things have I written unto you that believe on the name of the Son of God; that ye may know that ye have eternal life." — 1 John 5:13

New believers should understand that salvation rests on:

- God's grace
- Christ's finished work
- faith in Jesus

Assurance stabilizes faith and protects against discouragement.

Helping New Believers Understand What Has Happened

After conversion, questions naturally arise:

- What does it mean to be saved?
- What has changed?
- How should life look now?

Care includes explaining:

- forgiveness of sin
- new identity in Christ
- the indwelling presence of the Holy Spirit
- the call to follow Jesus

Clarity replaces confusion and strengthens spiritual foundations.

Introducing the Spiritual Disciplines

Spiritual growth does not occur automatically. New believers must be gently introduced to practices that nurture faith and deepen relationship with God.

Foundational disciplines include:

- prayer
- reading Scripture
- worship
- fellowship with believers
- obedience

These disciplines are means of grace, not burdens. They shape habits that sustain long-term growth.

The Importance of Christian Community

Salvation brings individuals into the family of God. Isolation weakens faith; community strengthens it.

"And they continued stedfastly in the apostles' doctrine and fellowship." — Acts 2:42

New believers need:

- encouragement
- accountability
- teaching
- spiritual example

Caring for new believers means ensuring they are **not left alone**.

Walking with New Believers Through Early Challenges

The early days of faith often include challenges:

- temptation
- misunderstanding
- opposition from others
- spiritual confusion

These struggles do not negate salvation; they are part of growth. Mature believers are called to walk patiently alongside new believers, offering truth and encouragement.

Guidance during this season helps prevent discouragement and spiritual drift.

From Convert to Disciple

Jesus did not command His followers to make converts, but disciples.

"Teaching them to observe all things whatsoever I have commanded you." — Matthew 28:20

Discipleship includes:

- learning Scripture
- developing Christlike character
- cultivating obedience
- understanding mission

The goal is not dependence on people, but dependence on Christ.

Preparing New Believers for Discipleship Training

Follow-up care should intentionally lead new believers into structured discipleship. Foundational training helps them understand:

- core Christian beliefs
- how to read the Bible
- how to pray
- how to live out faith daily

This preparation creates a natural transition into systematic discipleship, such as the **Equipped to Disciple** pathway, which builds maturity step by step.

Encouraging Early Witness

New believers often possess fresh joy and authentic testimony. With gentle guidance, they can begin sharing their faith naturally and responsibly.

Early encouragement helps new believers understand that:

- evangelism is part of discipleship
- testimony grows with maturity
- faith is strengthened through obedience

Faithful Care Reflects the Heart of God

God does not abandon those He saves. He nurtures, corrects, and sustains them.

"He shall feed his flock like a shepherd." — Isaiah 40:11

When the Church cares for new believers, it reflects God's shepherding heart. Evangelism reaches its fullness when those who believe are lovingly guided into maturity and mission.

Reflection Questions

1. Why is follow-up care essential after salvation?
2. What challenges commonly arise in the early days of faith?
3. How does assurance of salvation protect new believers?

Personal Assignments

- **Assignment 1 — Scripture Study:** Read John 10 and Romans 8. Identify promises that strengthen assurance.
- **Assignment 2 — Care Plan:** Write a simple plan for how you would support a new believer during their first month of faith.
- **Assignment 3 — Prayerful Commitment:** Commit to praying regularly for new believers God places in your life.

Ministry / Small-Group Assignments

- **Group Discussion:** Discuss common mistakes churches make in follow-up and how to avoid them.
- **Teaching Activity:** Create a basic follow-up checklist for new believers (prayer, Scripture, fellowship).
- **Group Prayer:** Pray for wisdom, patience, and love in nurturing new believers.

Prayer

Heavenly Father, Thank You for the miracle of salvation and new life in Christ. Teach us to care faithfully for those You bring into Your family. Give us wisdom to guide, patience to nurture, and love that reflects Your heart. Anchor new believers in truth, surround them with godly community, and lead them into spiritual maturity. May every soul saved be lovingly shepherded into a growing, fruitful life in Christ. In Jesus' name, Amen.

Chapter 14
Reflection & Notes Worksheet
Equipped to Evangelize

Chapter Title: The Moment After Salvation
Date: _____

Key Scriptures from This Chapter (Write the Bible verses that stood out most to you.)

_____
_____
_____
_____
_____
_____
_____

Main Truths & Key Insights (What were the most important teachings or ideas in this chapter?)

_____
_____
_____
_____
_____
_____
_____

Personal Reflection (How did this chapter challenge, encourage, or correct your thinking?)

_____
_____
_____
_____
_____
_____
_____

Application to My Life (What changes, actions, or attitudes does God want you to apply?)

_____

_____

_____

_____

_____

_____

Evangelism Focus (How does this chapter help you grow as a witness for Christ?)

_____

_____

_____

_____

_____

Prayer Response (Write a prayer in response to what you learned.

_____

_____

_____

_____

_____

_____

Questions I Still Have (Write any questions you want to study further or discuss.)

_____

_____

_____

_____

_____

_____

Action Step for This Week (One practical step you will take based on this chapter.)

_____

_____

_____

_____

_____

_____

_____

Additional Notes

_____

_____

_____

_____

_____

_____

_____

Discussion Notes / Group Insights:

_____

_____

_____

_____

_____

_____

_____

CHAPTER 15

Follow-Up, Church Connection, and Discipleship
Helping Converts Grow, Belong, and Mature

Salvation Leads to Belonging

God never intended salvation to be lived out in isolation. From the beginning, those who believed were gathered, taught, and formed into community. The gospel not only reconciles individuals to God; it **joins them to the people of God**.

"Now therefore ye are no more strangers and foreigners, but fellowcitizens with the saints, and of the household of God." — Ephesians 2:19

Follow-up care that does not lead to church connection leaves believers spiritually vulnerable and disconnected from God's design for growth.

Why Follow-Up Must Be Intentional

Many believers drift not because they rejected Christ, but because they were never guided after conversion. Scripture consistently shows that growth requires **intentional teaching and relationship**.

The early Church understood this clearly:
"And they continued stedfastly in the apostles' doctrine and fellowship." — Acts 2:42

Intentional follow-up:
- reinforces assurance
- builds spiritual habits
- provides accountability
- connects believers to community

Without structure, even sincere faith can stagnate.

The Local Church: God's Design for Growth

God's primary context for discipleship is the local church. While personal study and relationships matter, Scripture places teaching, fellowship, and accountability within the gathered body.

The church provides:

- biblical instruction
- pastoral care
- spiritual covering
- opportunities for service

Connection to the local church helps believers move from spiritual infancy toward maturity.

From New Believer to Growing Disciple

Discipleship is the process by which believers learn to follow Jesus in every area of life. It involves both **information and formation**.

Key areas of discipleship include:

- understanding Scripture
- developing prayer life
- learning obedience
- shaping Christlike character
- discovering purpose and mission

Discipleship is not rushed. It is walked out over time, with patience and grace.

The Need for Structured Discipleship

While informal mentoring is valuable, Scripture and experience show the effectiveness of **structured discipleship pathways**. Clear teaching helps believers build a strong foundation without confusion.

A structured approach:

- ensures doctrinal clarity
- establishes spiritual disciplines
- provides measurable growth
- supports consistent teaching

This structure protects new believers from misinformation and spiritual instability.

The Role of *Equipped to Disciple*

The *Equipped to Disciple* series was designed to serve precisely at this stage—providing a **clear, biblical, and practical pathway** for believers after conversion.

Through systematic teaching, *Equipped to Disciple* helps believers learn:
- the basics of Christian faith
- how to read and understand Scripture
- how to pray and worship
- how to live out obedience
- how to grow in character and service

This series supports churches, families, and small groups in nurturing consistent spiritual growth.

Discipleship Across Life Stages

Effective follow-up recognizes that discipleship is not one-size-fits-all. Age, maturity, and life context matter.

A comprehensive discipleship approach:
- adapts teaching to life stage
- reinforces core truths consistently
- encourages growth at every level

This ensures that believers are not only converted, but continually formed into faithful disciples.

Accountability and Encouragement

Growth flourishes where encouragement and accountability walk together. Discipleship relationships provide space for questions, correction, and celebration.

"Exhort one another daily." — Hebrews 3:13

Healthy accountability:
- strengthens perseverance
- prevents isolation
- nurtures spiritual maturity

Discipleship is not control; it is care.

Discipleship Leads to Multiplication

True discipleship always looks outward. As believers grow, they are called not only to follow Christ, but to help others follow Him.

"The things that thou hast heard of me... commit thou to faithful men." — 2 Timothy 2:2

Evangelism and discipleship form a continuous cycle:

- evangelism leads to discipleship
- discipleship produces maturity
- maturity leads to multiplication

The Church grows strongest when this cycle remains unbroken.

Guarding Against Disconnection

When believers are not guided into discipleship, several risks arise:
- spiritual stagnation
- doctrinal confusion
- vulnerability to false teaching
- disengagement from church life

Intentional follow-up protects against these dangers and honors God's design.

A Faith That Grows Deep and Lasts Long

Discipleship ensures that faith is not built on emotion alone, but on truth, obedience, and relationship. The goal is not temporary enthusiasm, but **lifelong faithfulness**.
Evangelism reaches maturity when believers are rooted, growing, and connected.

Reflection Questions
1. Why is church connection essential after salvation?
2. How does structured discipleship support long-term spiritual growth?
3. In what ways does discipleship prepare believers for multiplication?

Personal Assignments

- **Assignment 1 — Church Connection:** Identify specific ways a new believer can become meaningfully connected to a local church.
- **Assignment 2 — Discipleship Commitment:** Commit to engaging in or supporting a structured discipleship pathway such as *Equipped to Disciple*.
- **Assignment 3 — Prayerful Support:** Pray regularly for believers in your church who are early in their faith journey.

Ministry / Small-Group Assignments

- **Group Discussion:** Discuss how churches can strengthen follow-up and discipleship systems.
- **Teaching Activity:** Create a simple discipleship roadmap for new believers in your ministry.
- **Group Prayer:** Pray for unity, wisdom, and faithfulness in guiding believers toward maturity.

Prayer

Heavenly Father, Thank You for placing us within Your Church and calling us to grow together. Teach us to care faithfully for those You save, guiding them into community, truth, and maturity. Bless every effort to disciple believers according to Your Word. May our churches be places where faith is nurtured, truth is taught, and lives are transformed for Your glory. In Jesus' name, Amen.

Chapter 15
Reflection & Notes Worksheet
Equipped to Evangelize

Chapter Title: Follow-Up, Church Connection, and Discipleship
Date: _____

Key Scriptures from This Chapter (Write the Bible verses that stood out most to you.)

_____
_____
_____
_____
_____
_____
_____

Main Truths & Key Insights (What were the most important teachings or ideas in this chapter?)

_____
_____
_____
_____
_____
_____
_____

Personal Reflection (How did this chapter challenge, encourage, or correct your thinking?)

_____
_____
_____
_____
_____
_____
_____

Application to My Life (What changes, actions, or attitudes does God want you to apply?)

Evangelism Focus (How does this chapter help you grow as a witness for Christ?)

Prayer Response (Write a prayer in response to what you learned.

Questions I Still Have (Write any questions you want to study further or discuss.)

Action Step for This Week (One practical step you will take based on this chapter.)

_____
_____
_____
_____
_____
_____
_____

Additional Notes

_____
_____
_____
_____
_____
_____

Discussion Notes / Group Insights:

_____
_____
_____
_____
_____
_____

CHAPTER 16

Evangelism as a Lifestyle
Living Sent Every Day

From Event to Identity

Evangelism was never meant to be an occasional activity reserved for special events or gifted individuals. In Scripture, evangelism flows from **identity**, not scheduling. To follow Christ is to be sent by Christ.

"As my Father hath sent me, even so send I you." — John 20:21

When evangelism is reduced to an event, it becomes optional. When evangelism is embraced as identity, it becomes natural.

Believers do not turn evangelism on and off; they **live sent**.

A Gospel-Shaped Way of Life

Evangelism as a lifestyle means allowing the gospel to shape how believers:

- speak
- listen
- work
- serve
- respond to others

The gospel is not merely proclaimed; it is embodied. A gospel-shaped life reflects humility, compassion, integrity, and hope.

"Let your light so shine before men." — Matthew 5:16

Consistency over time builds credibility and invites curiosity.

Everyday Faithfulness Matters

God works powerfully through ordinary obedience. Many gospel moments occur quietly—through patience, kindness, honesty, and prayerful presence. Scripture reminds believers that God values faithfulness more than visibility.

"Moreover it is required in stewards, that a man be found faithful." — 1 Corinthians 4:2

Seeds planted faithfully often bear fruit long after the moment has passed.

Seeing Life Through a Missional Lens

Living sent requires learning to see everyday life as sacred opportunity rather than interruption. Conversations, responsibilities, and challenges become contexts for witness.

A missional lens asks:
- Where is God already at work?
- Who has God placed in my life?
- How can I reflect Christ here?

This perspective transforms routine into purpose.

Balancing Boldness and Wisdom

Evangelism as a lifestyle does not mean constant talking. It means **faithful readiness**—speaking when God opens doors and listening when He calls for patience.

"Walk in wisdom toward them that are without." — Colossians 4:5

Boldness without wisdom can harm witness. Wisdom without boldness can silence it. The Holy Spirit unites both.

Perseverance in the Long Journey

Evangelism is rarely a straight line. Rejection, delays, and discouragement are part of the journey. Living sent means continuing faithfully even when results are unseen.

"In due season we shall reap, if we faint not." — Galatians 6:9

God measures success by obedience, not immediacy.

Evangelism and Discipleship Remain United

A lifestyle of evangelism never stands alone; it flows naturally into discipleship. Those who believe are guided into growth, community, and maturity.

The cycle continues:
- the gospel is shared
- believers are discipled
- disciples live sent
- others hear and respond

This rhythm sustains the mission of the Church across generations.

Depending on God Daily

Living sent requires continual dependence on God. Prayer, Scripture, and fellowship remain essential—not as duties, but as lifelines.

Daily dependence keeps the evangelist:
- humble rather than proud
- patient rather than pressured
- faithful rather than fearful

God supplies strength for every step.

The Church as a Sent Community

When individuals live sent, the Church becomes a sent community. Evangelism ceases to be a program and becomes a shared culture.

A sent church:
- welcomes seekers
- nurtures believers
- equips disciples
- sends witnesses

This culture honors Christ and fulfills His mission.

A Final Commissioning

As this book concludes, the calling remains. The mission did not end with the early Church, nor does it end with reading these pages. Christ still sends His people into the world with the same authority, the same message, and the same promise of His presence.

"And, lo, I am with you alway, even unto the end of the world." — Matthew 28:20

You are sent—not because you are perfect, but because Christ is faithful.

Reflection Questions
1. How does viewing evangelism as identity change daily life?
2. What habits help sustain a lifestyle of faithful witness?
3. In what ways can perseverance strengthen long-term evangelism?

Personal Assignments

- **Assignment 1 — Missional Reflection:** Write a brief statement describing how you will live sent in your daily context.
- **Assignment 2 — Lifestyle Commitment:** Identify one habit that will help you remain spiritually prepared for evangelism.
- **Assignment 3 — Prayerful Dependence:** Commit to daily prayer, asking God to guide your words, actions, and attitudes.

Ministry / Small-Group Assignments

- **Group Discussion:** Discuss how churches can cultivate evangelism as a lifestyle rather than a program.
- **Teaching Activity:** Create a simple plan for integrating evangelism and discipleship in everyday church life.
- **Group Prayer:** Pray for unity, obedience, and faithfulness as a sent community.

Final Prayer of Commissioning

Heavenly Father, We thank You for the gospel that has saved us and the mission You have entrusted to us. As we go from here, teach us to live sent every day. Fill us with Your Spirit, guide our steps, and guard our hearts. Help us walk faithfully, speak truth lovingly, and trust You completely. May our lives proclaim the hope of Jesus Christ wherever You place us. In His name we pray, Amen.

Chapter 16
Reflection & Notes Worksheet
Equipped to Evangelize

Chapter Title: Evangelism as a Lifestyle
Date: _____

Key Scriptures from This Chapter (Write the Bible verses that stood out most to you.)

_____
_____
_____
_____
_____
_____
_____

Main Truths & Key Insights (What were the most important teachings or ideas in this chapter?)

_____
_____
_____
_____
_____
_____
_____

Personal Reflection (How did this chapter challenge, encourage, or correct your thinking?)

_____
_____
_____
_____
_____
_____
_____

Application to My Life (What changes, actions, or attitudes does God want you to apply?)

_____
_____
_____
_____
_____
_____

Evangelism Focus (How does this chapter help you grow as a witness for Christ?)

_____
_____
_____
_____
_____

Prayer Response (Write a prayer in response to what you learned.

_____
_____
_____
_____
_____
_____

Questions I Still Have (Write any questions you want to study further or discuss.)

_____
_____
_____
_____
_____
_____

Action Step for This Week (One practical step you will take based on this chapter.)

_____

_____

_____

_____

_____

_____

_____

Additional Notes

_____

_____

_____

_____

_____

_____

Discussion Notes / Group Insights:

_____

_____

_____

_____

_____

_____

CONCLUSION & FINAL COMMISSIONING

Sent by God, Sustained by Grace

From Knowledge to Obedience

This book was never meant to end in information alone. Evangelism is not mastered by reading, studying, or agreeing—it is fulfilled by **obedience**. From the heart of God for the lost to the daily calling to live sent, every chapter has pointed toward one central truth: **the gospel is entrusted to God's people to be lived and proclaimed**.

The question at the conclusion is not *¿What have you learned?* It is *¿How will you live?*

The gospel moves forward not through perfect messengers, but through faithful ones.

The Unchanging Gospel in a Changing World

Methods evolve. Cultures shift. Technologies advance. But the gospel remains the same. Jesus Christ—crucified, risen, and reigning—continues to be the hope of the world.

God has chosen to make His appeal through ordinary believers in ordinary places. This has always been His design. The power of evangelism does not lie in strategy, personality, or eloquence, but in the **Spirit of God working through surrendered lives**.

You were not saved merely to be rescued from sin. You were saved to be **sent**.

You Are Already Positioned by God

You do not need to wait for a title, platform, or permission to begin living as a witness. God has already positioned you—within your family, workplace, school, community, and relationships.

- Every conversation carries potential.
- Every act of love bears witness.
- Every faithful step of obedience matters.

The mission field is not only "out there." It is where you already live.

Faithfulness, Not Fear, Defines the Evangelist

Fear will always attempt to silence obedience. Insecurity will always whisper that you are not ready or not enough.

But Scripture consistently reveals that God works most powerfully through those who trust Him beyond themselves.

- You are not called to save anyone.
- You are called to **testify**.
- You are not responsible for outcomes.
- You are responsible for **obedience**.

God gives the increase.

Evangelism Sustained by Grace

Evangelism is not sustained by pressure, guilt, or performance. It is sustained by grace. Grace reminds believers that:

- God works before, during, and after every conversation
- failure does not disqualify obedience
- perseverance matters more than immediate results

When evangelism flows from gratitude rather than obligation, it becomes joyful rather than burdensome.

A Call to Lifelong Faithfulness

Evangelism is not a season—it is a calling that lasts a lifetime. There will be moments of fruit and moments of waiting. Times of boldness and times of quiet faithfulness. God is present in all of them.

- Some seeds will be planted.
- Some will be watered.
- Some will be harvested by others.

All faithful obedience is seen and honored by God.

Final Commissioning

As this book concludes, the call remains clear and unchanged:
"Go ye into the entire world, and preach the gospel to every creature."

This is not merely a command to remember—it is a commission to **live**.

You are commissioned to:

- live anchored in the gospel
- speak truth with grace
- love people with compassion
- trust the Holy Spirit fully
- stand firm in faith
- walk with new believers patiently
- remain faithful regardless of response

A Prayer of Commissioning

Heavenly Father, Thank You for the gospel of Jesus Christ—the power of salvation for all who believe. Thank You for calling ordinary people to carry an extraordinary message. As this journey of learning concludes, a journey of obedience begins.
We surrender fear, insecurity, and self-reliance. We receive Your grace, Your Spirit, and Your calling. Send us into our homes, communities, workplaces, and the world as faithful witnesses of Christ. Teach us to live sent every day—humble, bold, compassionate, and obedient. May our lives reflect Your love, our words proclaim Your truth, and our faithfulness bring glory to Your name. Use us for Your purposes, in Your timing, for Your glory alone. In the name of Jesus Christ, Amen.

Final Charge

Go with confidence.
Go with compassion.
Go with humility.
Go with courage.

You are equipped.
You are called.
You are sent.

APPENDICES

APPENDIX A — A Simple Gospel Outline
A Ready-to-Use Presentation
This gospel outline is designed to be **clear, biblical, and adaptable**. It may be shared in personal conversations, outreach events, hospital visits, homes, schools, or churches.

1. God's Original Design
God created humanity for relationship with Himself, to live in love, holiness, and purpose.
Scriptures
- Genesis 1:27
- Isaiah 43:7

2. Humanity's Problem: Sin
Sin separates humanity from God and brings spiritual death. No one is exempt.
Scriptures
- Romans 3:23
- Romans 6:23

3. God's Loving Provision: Jesus Christ
God sent His Son, Jesus Christ, who lived without sin, died for our sins, and rose again.
Scriptures
- Romans 5:8
- 1 Corinthians 15:3–4

4. Our Response: Repentance and Faith
Salvation is received by turning from sin and trusting in Jesus Christ alone.
Scriptures
- Acts 3:19
- Romans 10:9–10

5. God's Promise

Those who believe are forgiven, made new, and receive eternal life.

Scriptures
- John 1:12
- 2 Corinthians 5:17

Closing Invitation

Would you like to place your trust in Jesus Christ today?

APPENDIX B — Key Scriptures on Evangelism and the Holy Spirit

These Scriptures strengthen confidence in evangelism and emphasize **dependence on the Holy Spirit**, not human ability.

The Call to Evangelize
- Matthew 28:19–20
- Mark 16:15
- Acts 1:8

The Role of the Holy Spirit
- John 16:8 – Conviction of sin
- Acts 4:31 – Boldness through the Spirit
- Zechariah 4:6 – Not by might, but by God's Spirit

God's Heart for the Lost
- Luke 19:10
- 1 Timothy 2:3–4
- 2 Peter 3:9

Confidence in God's Work
- 1 Corinthians 3:6–7
- Isaiah 55:11
- Philippians 1:6

APPENDIX C — Sample Evangelism Prayers
Depending on the Spirit in Witness

These examples of prayers may be used **before, during, and after evangelism**, personally or corporately.

Prayer Before Evangelizing

"Holy Spirit, guide my steps and my words. Open hearts and prepare divine appointments. Help me speak truth with love and boldness. I trust You to do what only You can do. In Jesus' name, Amen."

Prayer During a Gospel Conversation

"Lord, give wisdom, patience, and compassion. Remove fear and let Your truth be clear. May Your Spirit work in this heart. In Jesus' name, Amen."

Prayer After Sharing the Gospel

"Father, I place this person in Your hands. Continue the work You have begun. Let Your Word take root and bear fruit in Your time. In Jesus' name, Amen."

Prayer for New Believers

"Lord, strengthen this new believer. Anchor them in truth, surround them with godly community, and lead them into spiritual growth and discipleship. In Jesus' name, Amen."

APPENDIX D — Small Group & Training Guide
Church and Classroom Use
This guide helps pastors, teachers, and leaders use *Equipped to Evangelize* in **group settings**

Suggested 8-Week Training Plan

Week 1: The Heart of God for the Lost
Week 2: The Gospel Message Clearly Explained
Week 3: The Role of the Holy Spirit in Evangelism
Week 4: Overcoming Fear and Insecurity
Week 5: Responding to Questions and Objections
Week 6: Rejection, Opposition, and Perseverance
Week 7: Caring for New Believers & Follow-Up
Week 8: Evangelism as a Lifestyle

This 8-week training plan is a foundational pathway designed to introduce believers to the essential principles of evangelism. Readers are strongly encouraged to continue studying the remaining chapters for deeper formation, specialized application, and long-term discipleship."

Group Session Structure
1. Opening Prayer
2. Scripture Reading
3. Teaching from the chapter
4. Group Discussion
5. Practical Assignment
6. Closing Prayer

Practical Training Activities
- Role-play gospel conversations
- Practice sharing personal testimonies
- Scripture memorization
- Group prayer for the lost
- Community outreach planning

Recommended Follow-Up

After completing this book, groups are encouraged to continue with the *Equipped to Disciple* **series** to ensure lasting spiritual growth and multiplication.

FINAL NOTE
These appendices are tools—not substitutes for the Holy Spirit. Use them prayerfully, faithfully, and with compassion.

Be equipped to evangelize.
Be equipped to disciple.

Glossary

Assurance of Salvation: Confidence that one is saved, based on God's promises and Christ's finished work, not on feelings or performance (1 John 5:11–13).

Born Again: The spiritual rebirth that occurs when a person places faith in Jesus Christ and receives new life through the Holy Spirit (John 3:3–7).

Calling: God's invitation and purpose for believers to follow Christ and live according to His will, including participation in His mission.

Church: The body of believers united in Christ, both universally and locally, established for worship, teaching, fellowship, and mission (Ephesians 2:19–22).

Compassion: Christlike concern for others that moves believers to act in love, mercy, and truth, especially toward the lost and suffering.

Conversion: The moment a person turns from sin and places faith in Jesus Christ, resulting in salvation and reconciliation with God (Acts 3:19).

Conviction: The work of the Holy Spirit in revealing sin, righteousness, and the need for salvation (John 16:8).

Cross: The instrument of Jesus Christ's death, where He bore the penalty for sin and accomplished redemption for humanity (1 Peter 2:24).

Discipleship: The lifelong process of learning, obeying, and becoming more like Jesus Christ, including spiritual growth and multiplication (Matthew 28:19–20).

Evangelism: The act of sharing the gospel of Jesus Christ through words and actions, inviting others to repentance and faith.

Faith: Trust and reliance upon Jesus Christ alone for salvation and daily living (Ephesians 2:8–9).

Forgiveness: God's gracious act of removing sin and guilt through the sacrifice of Jesus Christ (Colossians 1:13–14).

Gospel: The good news that Jesus Christ died for our sins, was buried, and rose again, offering salvation to all who believe (1 Corinthians 15:3–4).

Grace: God's unearned favor toward humanity, through which salvation and spiritual growth are made possible (Romans 5:1–2).

Great Commission: Jesus' command to His followers to make disciples of all nations by proclaiming the gospel and teaching obedience to His Word (Matthew 28:19–20).

Holy Spirit: The third Person of the Trinity, who convicts of sin, empowers believers, guides truth, and produces spiritual fruit (John 16:13; Acts 1:8).

Justification: God's declaration that a believer is righteous through faith in Jesus Christ, not by works (Romans 5:1).

New Birth. Another term for being born again; the spiritual transformation that begins a new life in Christ.

Obedience: Faithful submission to God's will and commands as an expression of love and trust in Him (John 14:15).

Prayer: Communication with God that includes praise, confession, thanksgiving, and requests, sustained by faith and dependence on Him.

Redemption: The act of being delivered from sin and death through the blood of Jesus Christ (Ephesians 1:7).

Repentance: A change of mind and direction that turns away from sin and toward God (Acts 2:38).

Salvation: God's gift of deliverance from sin and eternal separation through faith in Jesus Christ (Romans 10:9–10).

Sanctification: The ongoing process by which believers grow in holiness and become more like Christ through the Holy Spirit (1 Thessalonians 4:3).

Scripture: The inspired Word of God, given as the authoritative guide for faith, doctrine, and life (2 Timothy 3:16).

Sin: Any thought, word, or action that falls short of God's holy standard and separates humanity from Him (Romans 3:23).

Spiritual Disciplines: Practices such as prayer, Bible study, worship, and fellowship that help believers grow in faith and obedience.

Spiritual Warfare: The ongoing spiritual conflict between God's truth and the forces of darkness, in which believers stand firm through faith and obedience (Ephesians 6:10–18).

Testimony: A personal account of how God has worked in one's life, especially in salvation and transformation (Revelation 12:11).

Trinity: The biblical doctrine that God exists as one God in three Persons: Father, Son, and Holy Spirit.

Witness: A believer's calling to testify to the truth of Jesus Christ through life, words, and actions (Acts 1:8).

Final Note

This glossary is provided to strengthen understanding, encourage clarity, and support both new believers and seasoned Christians as they grow in faith and confidence in evangelism.

Bibliography
Primary Source
The Holy Bible.

King James Version (KJV). Public Domain. (Unless otherwise noted, all Scripture quotations are from the King James Version.)

Biblical Theology & Doctrine
Bruce, F. F. *The Canon of Scripture.* Downers Grove, IL: InterVarsity Press, 1988.

Erickson, Millard J. *Christian Theology.* 3rd ed. Grand Rapids, MI: Baker Academic, 2013.

Grudem, Wayne. *Systematic Theology: An Introduction to Biblical Doctrine.* Grand Rapids, MI: Zondervan, 1994.

Horton, Stanley M. *What the Bible Says About the Holy Spirit.* Springfield, MO: Gospel Publishing House, 1976.

Packer, J. I. *Knowing God.* Downers Grove, IL: InterVarsity Press, 1973.

Evangelism & Mission
Coleman, Robert E. *The Master Plan of Evangelism.* Rev. ed. Grand Rapids, MI: Baker Books, 2006.

Green, Michael. *Evangelism in the Early Church.* Rev. ed. Grand Rapids, MI: Eerdmans, 2004.

Piper, John. *Let the Nations Be Glad!* 3rd ed. Grand Rapids, MI: Baker Academic, 2010.

Stott, John R. W. *Christian Mission in the Modern World.* Downers Grove, IL: InterVarsity Press, 2008.

Wagner, C. Peter. *Church Growth and the Whole Gospel.* San Francisco, CA: Harper & Row, 1981.

Discipleship & Spiritual Formation

Bonhoeffer, Dietrich. *The Cost of Discipleship.* New York, NY: Touchstone, 1995.

Hull, Bill. *The Disciple-Making Church.* Rev. ed. Grand Rapids, MI: Baker Books, 2010.

Willard, Dallas. *The Great Omission.* San Francisco, CA: HarperOne, 2006.

Wilkins, Michael J. *Following the Master: A Biblical Theology of Discipleship.* Grand Rapids, MI: Zondervan, 1992.

The Holy Spirit & Christian Living

Fee, Gordon D. *Paul, the Spirit, and the People of God.* Peabody, MA: Hendrickson, 1996.

Tozer, A. W. *The Divine Conquest.* Camp Hill, PA: Christian Publications, 1950.

Tozer, A. W. *How to Be Filled with the Holy Spirit.* Minneapolis, MN: Bethany House, 1964.

Apologetics & Responding to Objections

McDowell, Josh. *Evidence That Demands a Verdict.* Rev. ed. Nashville, TN: Thomas Nelson, 1999.

Strobel, Lee. *The Case for Christ.* Grand Rapids, MI: Zondervan, 1998.

Sproul, R. C. *Reason to Believe.* Grand Rapids, MI: Zondervan, 1978.

Pastoral Care & Church Life

MacArthur, John. *The Gospel According to Jesus.* Rev. ed. Grand Rapids, MI: Zondervan, 2008.

Peterson, Eugene H. *A Long Obedience in the Same Direction.* Downers Grove, IL: InterVarsity Press, 2000.

Warren, Rick. *The Purpose Driven Church.* Grand Rapids, MI: Zondervan, 1995.

Spiritual Warfare & Perseverance

Arnold, Clinton E. *3 Crucial Questions About Spiritual Warfare.* Grand Rapids, MI: Baker Books, 1997.

Prince, Derek. *Spiritual Warfare.* Grand Rapids, MI: Chosen Books, 2006.

Discipleship Series Reference

Archbold, Frank S. *Equipped to Disciple.* Orlando, FL: F. S. Archbold Publishing LLC. (Used as a complementary discipleship pathway for follow-up and spiritual formation.)

Church History & Early Christianity

Eusebius. *The History of the Church.* Translated by G. A. Williamson. London: Penguin Classics, 1989.

Latourette, Kenneth Scott. *A History of Christianity.* Vol. 1. New York, NY: Harper & Row, 1953.

Final Note

This bibliography reflects a **biblical, evangelical, and discipleship-focused framework**, supporting the theological foundations and practical applications presented in *Equipped to Evangelize*. It is provided to encourage further study, faithful teaching, and lifelong growth in gospel ministry.

About the Author

Dr. Frank S. Archbold, Th.D., Ph.D. is a Christian theologian, author, educator, and ministry leader committed to equipping believers for faithful discipleship and effective witness in today's world. With decades of pastoral and academic experience, Dr. Archbold brings together sound biblical scholarship, practical ministry application, and a deep love for the Church and the nations. He is the founder of **F. S. Archbold Publishing LLC**, through which he develops biblically grounded resources for churches, families, schools, and ministry leaders. His widely used *Equipped to...* series provides structured, age-appropriate discipleship materials spanning children, youth, and adults, designed to foster spiritual formation, biblical literacy, and missional living across generations.

Dr. Archbold has served in diverse leadership roles within ecclesial, educational, and community contexts in the United States and Latin America. His work reflects a strong commitment to pastoral care, evangelism, Christian education, and community transformation, particularly in urban and underserved settings. He is also actively involved in developing educational initiatives and community programs that integrate faith, character formation, and practical life skills.

A bilingual communicator in English and Spanish, Dr. Archbold writes with clarity, theological depth, and pastoral sensitivity. His teaching emphasizes the authority of Scripture, the work of the Holy Spirit, and the call of every believer to live out the Great Commission with wisdom, compassion, and integrity.

Dr. Frank S. Archbold resides between ministry and educational initiatives, continuing to write, teach, and mentor leaders with the conviction that when believers are well equipped in the Word of God, families are strengthened, churches are built up, and communities are transformed for the glory of God.

Note:

Use your mobile device to scan this QR code, which will redirect you to the template document for printing the certificate of completion of discipleship.

www.ingramcontent.com/pod-product-compliance
Lightning Source LLC
Chambersburg PA
CBHW030258130626
46549CB00002B/584